# Opening the Door to
## Coaching
## CONVERSATIONS

**Linda Gross Cheliotes**     **Marceta Fleming Reilly**

with associates of Coaching For Results Global

# Opening the Door to
# Coaching
# CONVERSATIONS

Foreword by **Joellen Killion**

**CORWIN**
A SAGE Company

## CORWIN
A SAGE Company

FOR INFORMATION:

Corwin

A SAGE Company

2455 Teller Road

Thousand Oaks, California 91320

(800) 233-9936

www.corwin.com

SAGE Publications Ltd.

1 Oliver's Yard

55 City Road

London EC1Y 1SP

United Kingdom

SAGE Publications India Pvt. Ltd.

B 1/I 1 Mohan Cooperative Industrial Area

Mathura Road, New Delhi 110 044

India

SAGE Publications Asia-Pacific Pte. Ltd.

3 Church Street

#10-04 Samsung Hub

Singapore 049483

Acquisitions Editor:   Arnis Burvikovs

Associate Editor:   Desirée A. Bartlett

Editorial Assistant:   Kimberly Greenberg

Production Editor:   Amy Schroller

Copy Editor:   Diane DiMura

Typesetter:   C&M Digitals (P) Ltd.

Proofreader:   Gail Fay

Indexer:   Sylvia Coates

Cover Designer:   Karine Hovsepian

Permissions Editor:   Karen Ehrmann

All coaching skills emphasized in this book are from Coaching For Results, Inc. (2011). *Coaching strategies for powerful leading.* Hoyt, KS: Coaching For Results, Inc., also doing business as Coaching For Results Global.

Printed in the United States of America

A catalog record of this book is available from the Library of Congress.

ISBN 978-1-4522-0257-0

This book is printed on acid-free paper.

Certified Chain of Custody
Promoting Sustainable Forestry
www.sfiprogram.org
SFI-01268

SUSTAINABLE FORESTRY INITIATIVE

SFI label applies to text stock

12 13 14 15 16 10 9 8 7 6 5 4 3 2 1

# Contents

# Foreword

Artists for thousands of years have conveyed messages through their selected medium. Ancient cave painters ground pigments into rock to depict scenes from their lives. Hellenic potters used black slip and careful etchings of warriors, geometric shapes, and later more elaborate faces and figures. Renaissance painters made light dance out of dark canvases with their use of color. Other artists followed, each working in a medium to convey a message, inspire an observer, engage a viewer, and promote reflection.

New media artists take a different approach to art. Many work in multimedia rather than a single medium as earlier artists did. They select their media to underscore their message or to feature the beauty of what exists. Living artist Deborah Butterfield sculpts and casts exquisite horses from driftwood, and Clare Graham constructs art from found objects such as buttons, bottle caps, scrabble tiles, yardsticks, and pop tops. These common everyday objects take on new form and meaning beyond their essence at the hand of the artist.

Marcel Duchamp (1887–1968), a French artist considered to be among the most important artists of the 20th century, took a unique approach to his art for a period. He substituted for his own work ready-made objects, either alone, assembled, or constructed from other objects. Some of his more famous readymades included a bicycle wheel, comb, bottle rack, and typewriter cover. He chose ordinary, familiar objects and displayed them so they held new significance through their unique point of view. By withdrawing the artist from the art, Duchamp engaged the observer in personal and unpredictable ways. He allowed the observer to take an active role in the process of experiencing art. Duchamp believed that art emerged from the intersection of the artist's intention and the observer's response to the work as the observer became a partner in the meaning-making experience.

Duchamp's exploration with art signals how the authors in this book use the readymade of conversation to provoke, inspire, engage, and create art at the intersection of the coach and client. Words and conversations are everywhere. We use them to convey greetings, to order online and in restaurants, to comfort, to express feelings, to learn, and to conduct business. Because conversations are ubiquitous, appreciating the meaning and value of them is challenging. Yet when a coach takes the familiar, a conversation, and shares it in a new way, possibilities emerge. If the coach then engages the client to become a partner in the experience, significance radiates.

As readers unpack the scenarios and conversations shared by experienced coaches and education leaders within this book, they are invited to reflect on how they use words combined artfully into conversations to promote personal and professional growth in their clients and colleagues. The authors model through the scenarios drawn from their experiences how leaders artfully construct conversations to move heads, hearts, and hands. The book depicts how change agents catalyze others to clarify their goals and take action to achieve them. Serving others in this way is both a gift and an opportunity for leaders. Leaders will study the scenarios as models of how conversations support others to reach their highest potential, to solve complex problems, to resolve conflict, to build relational trust, to achieve high standards and audacious goals, to serve others, and to create possibilities. As readers enjoy the scenarios and various perspectives shared by the authors, they will find themselves reflecting on how they use words combined artfully into conversations to promote personal and professional growth.

Coaching conversations are the medium of leaders as the authors convey throughout this book. They depict how conversations used in a new way, as a form of art that intends to inspire an observer, renews the importance of conversation as an art form. Coaches select the medium of words for their art because words are familiar, and they mold them as an artist does into a work of art that offers a new point of view to engage their clients as partners at the intersection of the artist's intention and the partner's experience.

—Joellen Killion
*Senior Consultant, Learning Forward*

# Preface

Often when we present our leadership workshops, a participant will challenge us, suggesting that being coach-like in responding to issues that arise at work is fine for "easy" problems—and when you have lots of time. But, they continue, in the *real* world, there is too little time and too much "stuff" going on to use these skills on a regular basis.

Our response is that we have hundreds of stories about *real* clients, facing *real* problems, who consistently use coach-like skills every day with huge success. Coach-leadership is "leading from behind" as I (Linda) say. It is focused on *building the capacity of others* to resolve their own issues. The irony is that as leaders focus on developing those around them, they earn the deep trust and loyalty of staff—deeper than if they were the experts, doing the work themselves. With high trust and rapport comes high achievement (Bryk & Schneider, 2002)!

Our purpose in writing *Opening the Door to Coaching Conversations*, then, is to share stories of *real* school leaders who are using these coach-like skills everyday in their work to resolve their most challenging issues. It is meant to be a companion to *Coaching Conversations: Transforming Your School One Conversation at a Time* (Cheliotes & Reilly, 2010) in order to provide readers with rich examples of coach-like skills in action. We want to make the case that coach-leadership is not only possible, it is the *smartest* way to lead in the 21st century!

## USING THIS BOOK

The first chapter is intended as a simplified summary of coaching conversational skills. For a fuller understanding of the four essential coaching skills, the authors refer you to *Coaching Conversations: Transforming Your School One Conversation at a Time*.

Each of the remaining chapters deals with a specific area of challenge faced by school personnel at all levels of the educational organization. It does not matter in what order these chapters are read. We have added a matrix of the included stories that summarizes the situation and describes the skills and coaching competencies used within each story so that you can read what resonates with you at a given time or when you are facing a specific challenge.

## Matrix of Stories

Within each chapter, you will find several true stories illustrating how coach-leaders have used coach-like skills to recognize and grow their own skills or to help others grow professionally. We have highlighted the essential coaching skills illustrated by the stories and provided space for you to journal your personal reflections, questions, intentions, and next steps. This journaling step is really the *most important* component of this book. The more intentional and reflective you are about *how you want to be* in your school, the more likely you will hold successful coaching conversations that engage yourself and others in deep reflection and meaningful dialogue. Your *state of being* includes your mindset, your emotions, your demeanor, and how you want others to perceive you. While you may be able to enforce short-term compliance in others, you have control only over your own state of being: how you think and act in any given situation. By being a coach-leader, you provide space for other people to grow and change, build trusting relationships, and engage in meaningful, respectful interactions.

For a more complete discussion of becoming a coach-leader and learning the essential coaching skills, we recommend reading *RESULTS Coaching: The New Essential for School Leaders* (Kee, Anderson, Dearing, Harris, & Shuster, 2010). Another excellent resource is *The Elementary Principal's Personal Coach* (Williams & Richardson, 2010).

## SOURCE OF STORIES FOR THIS BOOK

Our coach colleagues from Coaching For Results Global have written many of the exemplar stories in this book, and we are extremely grateful for their willingness and generosity in sharing the experiences of their clients who have successfully used coaching conversations and become coach-leaders in their school communities. While all stories are true, we have changed the names and certain details of coaching clients' stories to maintain their confidentiality. Our Coaching For Results Global associates are all experienced school leaders and coaches, and we invite you to learn more about these gifted individuals at www.coachingforresultsglobal.com.

## GETTING STARTED

Here is an exercise you can do right now to begin your practice of being a coach-leader. Consider your current status and that of your school. What are your greatest challenges? Do your expectations and vision match the reality? If you woke up tomorrow morning and during the night a magical change had occurred and you and your school were now exactly as you had envisioned them, what would be different? What would you see? What would you hear? How would people act? What would you touch first?

Journal below about these ideas and let your evolution to coach-leadership begin!

_____

_____

_____

_____

_____

_____

_____

_____

## Matrix of Stories

| Chapter | Story Title | Synopsis |
| --- | --- | --- |
| 1 | Coach-Leader Man—Feeding the Hunger | A district leader dreams big and initiates a culture change for his entire district. |
| 2 | From Terminator to Hope Builder | A superintendent addresses dissention on his BOE (board of education) by helping them clarify and focus their priorities. |
| | A Yearning for More | A principal wants to change math instruction at his school. He holds up standards and expectations to guide staff through the changes. |
| | Courage at the Core | A first-year principal changes a cherished school tradition. |
| | Leading With Your Core Values | A principal newly assigned to a school in academic trouble has to deal with a very inexperienced assistant principal. |
| 3 | Better Late Than Never | An assistant principal deals with a teacher with a long history of tardiness. |
| | Language Matters | A principal uses positive intent with staff to counterbalance feelings of isolation and underappreciation often found in large districts. |
| | The Safest Haven | A principal recognizes evidence of high trust for her school within the community. |
| | From Parent Intrusion to Parent Involvement | A principal helps build bridges between an assertive parent and a defensive teacher. |

| Coaching Skills | | | | | Coach-Leadership Skills | | | | | | |
| Listening | Paraphrasing | Positive Intent | Powerful Questions | Feedback | Trust | Vision | Expectations | Core Values | Purpose | Reframing | Collaboration |
|---|---|---|---|---|---|---|---|---|---|---|---|
| ● | ● | ● |  |  |  | ● | ● | ● | ● |  | ● |
| ● | ● | ● | ● |  | ● | ● |  | ● |  |  | ● |
| ● |  | ● |  | ● |  | ● |  | ● | ● |  |  |
| ● | ● | ● | ● |  |  |  |  | ● | ● | ● | ● |
| ● |  | ● |  | ● | ● | ● | ● |  |  |  | ● |
| ● |  | ● | ● |  | ● |  | ● |  |  | ● |  |
|  | ● | ● |  |  | ● | ● | ● | ● |  |  |  |
| ● | ● | ● |  | ● | ● | ● | ● |  |  | ● |  |
| ● |  | ● | ● |  | ● | ● | ● |  | ● | ● | ● |

*(Continued)*

(Continued)

| Matrix of Stories | | |
|---|---|---|
| **Chapter** | **Story Title** | **Synopsis** |
| 4 | Finding Your Leadership Voice | A new principal in a school with a veteran staff learns to lead without being a dictator. |
| | Being Contagious Makes You Better | A principal challenges her staff to use high quality lesson planning EVERY day. |
| | Turning Around a Failing School | A principal is assigned to a school which has failed to make Adequate Yearly Progress. She has to organize the staff to quickly make a collective difference for students. |
| 5 | I Want to . . . But | An assistant principal wants to become a principal, yet he is resistant to change. |
| | The Crucial "Aha" Moment | A principal overcomes resistance to change by working on herself. |
| | Changing a Relationship Through Language | A new principal learns that providing unexpected positive feedback opened the door to change. |
| | Acting Out My Future—Life Is Just a Performance | An assistant principal uses positive intent to encourage a challenging student to change. |
| 6 | Reflected Glory | A high school principal gains commitment from staff by showing his support of them in his actions. |
| | Scoring With the Music Teacher | A principal is challenged by a teacher who does not buy in to a new district policy. |

| Coaching Skills | | | | | Coach-Leadership Skills | | | | | | |
|---|---|---|---|---|---|---|---|---|---|---|---|
| Listening | Paraphrasing | Positive Intent | Powerful Questions | Feedback | Trust | Vision | Expectations | Core Values | Purpose | Reframing | Collaboration |
| ● |  | ● | ● |  |  | ● | ● | ● |  | ● | ● |
|  |  | ● | ● | ● |  | ● | ● |  |  |  |  |
| ● |  | ● | ● |  | ● |  | ● | ● |  | ● | ● |
|  | ● |  |  | ● | ● |  |  |  |  | ● |  |
|  | ● | ● | ● | ● |  |  | ● |  |  | ● | ● |
|  | ● | ● | ● |  |  |  | ● |  |  | ● | ● |
| ● |  | ● |  |  |  | ● | ● |  | ● | ● |  |
| ● |  | ● | ● |  |  | ● | ● | ● |  |  | ● |
| ● |  | ● | ● |  | ● | ● | ● |  |  | ● | ● |

(Continued)

(Continued)

| Matrix of Stories | | |
|---|---|---|
| **Chapter** | **Story Title** | **Synopsis** |
| | It's in the Details | A principal feels micromanaged by his supervisor and discovers he is doing the same with his staff. |
| | Change Happens One by One | An assistant superintendent changes the climate within a leadership team. |
| 7 | Moving Staff Up or Out | A new principal has some fierce conversations with a few of her staff members. |
| | Reflection: A Closer Look | A district leader uses reflective questions to understand his new program responsibilities. |
| | A Marginal Teacher Spurs the Evolution of a Coach-Leader | A principal gets improvement results when she focuses on staff strengths. |
| | Facing Our Dragons | A principal tackles problems with his secretary. |
| 8 | Softening Discipline at the Edges | A new principal finds her biggest challenge to be creating a discipline climate with which she could live. |
| | Caught in the Middle | A principal is caught in the middle of a dispute between a teacher and the school board. |
| | "Nobody at This School Gets Me!" | A principal works with a student who blames the school system for his anger and frustration. |
| 9 | Monkey Collector | A principal takes on responsibility to handle issues that really belong to others. |

| Coaching Skills | | | | | Coach-Leadership Skills | | | | | | |
|---|---|---|---|---|---|---|---|---|---|---|---|
| Listening | Paraphrasing | Positive Intent | Powerful Questions | Feedback | Trust | Vision | Expectations | Core Values | Purpose | Reframing | Collaboration |
| ● |  | ● |  |  | ● | ● | ● |  | ● | ● | ● |
| ● | ● | ● |  |  | ● | ● |  | ● | ● | ● | ● |
|  | ● | ● | ● |  | ● | ● | ● |  | ● |  | ● |
| ● |  |  | ● | ● | ● | ● |  |  | ● | ● |  |
|  |  | ● | ● | ● | ● |  | ● |  |  | ● | ● |
| ● |  |  | ● | ● | ● | ● | ● | ● |  |  |  |
| ● | ● | ● |  |  | ● | ● | ● | ● |  |  | ● |
| ● |  | ● |  | ● | ● |  | ● | ● | ● |  |  |
| ● | ● | ● |  |  | ● | ● | ● | ● |  | ● | ● |
| ● | ● | ● | ● |  |  |  | ● |  | ● |  | ● |

(Continued)

(Continued)

## Matrix of Stories

| Chapter | Story Title | Synopsis |
| --- | --- | --- |
| | Whose Problem—Whose Solution? | A new principal learns ways to handle staff issues without giving advice. |
| | Just Call Me Mom | A principal learns to communicate caring without becoming "mom." |
| | Middle School Under Attack | An area superintendent works with a principal to strengthen communication without being directive or giving advice. |
| 10 | Sitting on a Seesaw | A new technology director learns that her "being" is as important as her "doing" in both her professional and personal life. |
| | The 180-Degree Turnaround | A department chair learns how to reduce his stress with a challenging teacher. |
| | Reframing Balance | A principal has trouble sorting "important" tasks from "urgent" ones. |
| | Running in Circles | An assistant principal feels diminished by ratings she received on a leadership inventory. |
| 11 | Rewiring | A principal prepares his staff for his impending retirement. |
| | I Feel Like a Failure | An assistant principal feels trapped in a position she does not like. |
| | Investing in the Next Steps | A curriculum leader is feeling unfocused and directionless about her approaching retirement. |

| Coaching Skills | | | | | | Coach-Leadership Skills | | | | | |
|---|---|---|---|---|---|---|---|---|---|---|---|
| Listening | Paraphrasing | Positive Intent | Powerful Questions | Feedback | Trust | Vision | Expectations | Core Values | Purpose | Reframing | Collaboration |
| ● |  | ● | ● | ● | ● |  | ● |  |  | ● | ● |
| ● | ● | ● | ● |  | ● |  | ● |  |  | ● | ● |
| ● |  | ● | ● |  | ● | ● | ● |  |  | ● | ● |
| ● | ● | ● | ● |  |  | ● | ● | ● | ● |  | ● |
| ● | ● | ● | ● | ● | ● |  | ● | ● |  | ● | ● |
| ● |  | ● | ● |  |  | ● | ● | ● | ● | ● |  |
| ● | ● | ● |  | ● | ● | ● | ● |  |  | ● |  |
| ● | ● | ● | ● | ● | ● | ● | ● | ● | ● | ● | ● |
| ● | ● | ● | ● |  | ● | ● | ● | ● | ● | ● |  |
| ● | ● | ● | ● | ● |  | ● | ● |  |  | ● | ● |

# Acknowledgments

We would like to acknowledge the many people who have encouraged and supported us throughout the writing of *Opening the Door to Coaching Conversations.* Our family members, friends, and coaching colleagues have each supplied large measures of inspiration and cheered us on in times of doubt.

The constant caring, suggestions, and friendship of Corwin staff, especially from our editor, Arnis Burvikovs, and his assistant, Kimberly Greenberg, have made us feel heard and confident. We truly feel all whom we have met at Corwin have become part of our extended family.

We are indebted to Joellen Killion, not only for taking time from her "retirement" to write the foreword for our book, but also for inspiring us for years regarding the value of coaching educators.

A special thanks goes to our business associates at Coaching For Results Global. Partnering with them as coauthors to shape ideas and stories brought us energy and creativity. It made the book a joy for us to write!

Finally, to the school leaders across the United States who reviewed our book, we thank you for reinforcing our goal to support educators as they incorporate coach-like behaviors into their daily practice.

## PUBLISHER'S ACKNOWLEDGMENTS

Corwin would like to thank the following individuals for taking the time to provide their editorial insight:

Sean Beggin
Assistant Principal
Andover High School
Andover, MN

# About the Authors

 **Linda Gross Cheliotes, EdD, ACC,** has over forty years of successful educational experience, including fourteen years as a school administrator. As principal, she transformed her underperforming school to a National Blue Ribbon School of Excellence, and her school was recognized twice within five years as one of the ten best public schools in New Jersey. Linda was named a National Distinguished Principal in 2002 and holds a doctorate in Organizational Leadership.

Linda is the coauthor with Marceta Fleming Reilly of *Coaching Conversations: Transforming Your School One Conversation at a Time*, a bestselling book published by Corwin in 2010.

For the past five years, Linda has been a coach and trainer with Coaching For Results Global, a national consortium of school leadership coaches. She is also a member of their board of directors, serving as Chief of Projects. She was a founding member and coach for the National Association of Elementary School Principals' (NAESP) national principal mentor certification program. Linda is an Associate Certified Coach (ACC) with the International Coach Federation.

 **Marceta Fleming Reilly, PhD, PCC,** has forty-five years of experience in education, moving from teacher to principal to school superintendent in Kansas. Her vision and passion were to create schools that were welcoming to students and families and centers of learning and success for the entire community.

Marceta is now a leadership coach and has the Professional Certified Coach (PCC) credential from the International Coach Federation. She is a founding member of Coaching For Results Global and dedicated to partnering with school leaders who are doing transformational work. She uses coaching conversations to help her clients gain insight and confidence, and she helps build their capacity to be extraordinary leaders, based on their individual, innate strengths.

Marceta and Linda regularly conduct workshops about coaching conversations. They are frequent speakers at state and national conferences, and they have presented these ideas to international audiences as well.

# About the Contributors

*O*pening the Door to Coaching Conversations contains many coach-leader stories by very gifted and experienced coaches—our Coaching For Results Global associates. Each of the individuals listed here has contributed one or more stories from their extensive coaching experience. The stories they have written will provide you with a rich variety of challenges successfully met by their clients with the encouragement of their coaches.

All of our colleagues have a broad background in the field of education, and they have worked as teachers, superintendents, and every position in between. They have dedicated their lives to supporting coach-leaders in schools and school districts and are passionate about the field of coaching. In addition, all Coaching For Results Global associates either have or are working toward professional coach credentials from the International Coach Federation (ICF), the leading international organization for coaches. Credentialing from ICF is a rigorous process that requires on-going professional development and extensive hours of coaching experience. Associate Certified Coach (ACC) is the first level credential while Professional Certified Coach (PCC) is the second of three possible credential levels.

You are invited to visit the website for Coaching For Results Global (http://www.coachingforresultsglobal.com) to learn much more about our talented coaches and their accomplishments. Marceta and Linda feel privileged to be associated with such amazing colleagues.

**Karen Anderson, MEd, PCC,** is a professional coach and learning facilitator who is passionate about coaching educators to higher levels of performance. She is a founding member of Coaching For Results Global and is currently responsible for the Teaching and

Learning Division. Karen is a coauthor of *RESULTS Coaching* (Corwin, 2010) and has authored numerous articles including "Coaching for High Performance" and "Leadership Coaching for Principals."

Bob Carter, MEd, specializes in coaching energetic, motivated school leaders who feel isolated, stressed out, and overworked. For over thirty-five years he has devoted his entire professional career to leadership development and coaching others for performance improvement. Coaching is Bob's way of providing on-going, just-in-time professional development that contributes to improved student performance in his clients' schools.

Sandee Crowther, EdD, ACC, is an experienced leadership coach and consultant, with a passion for helping leaders be the best they can be. She earned her doctorate in educational administration from the University of Kansas and worked for forty-three years in urban public schools in various roles. Sandee has received many significant educational honors including being immediate past president of Phi Delta Kappa International and a past president of the National Staff Development Council (now Learning Forward).

Vicky Dearing, MEd, PCC, is an experienced leadership coach and independent consultant with more than thirty-seven combined years of successful experience in both public education and the business sector. She has been recognized at the district, state, and national levels, including being the principal of two National Blue Ribbon Schools of Excellence. Recently, Vicky coauthored *RESULTS Coaching* (Corwin, 2010) and serves as the chief of marketing for Coaching For Results Global.

Edna Harris, MEd, PCC, is a founding member of Coaching For Results Global and coauthored *RESULTS Coaching* (Corwin, 2010). She has experience as a teacher, supervisor, reading coordinator, principal, and staff developer. She was named Texas Staff Developer of the Year in 1997 and has served on a variety of national and state task forces designed to promote effective staff development practices including teacher certification and legislative policies.

Joan Hearne, MEd, is currently a consultant and leadership coach in Wichita, Kansas, serving clients throughout the United States. As an educator in both urban and suburban school districts for over thirty years, she has experience as a middle school teacher, assistant principal, curriculum developer, staff development coordinator, behavior interventionist, elementary principal, and adjunct professor at Wichita State University. Joan has served as president of the Kansas Staff Development Council and was selected as Staff Developer of the Year.

**Kathy Kee, MEd, PCC,** is the lead author of *RESULTS Coaching* (Corwin, 2010), a successful school leader for over forty years, and a national trainer for Cognitive Coaching; Adaptive Schools; Carolyn Downey's Walk Through for Reflective Practice; Supervisory Language for Accelerating Results, with Dr. John Crain; mentoring and coaching skills, communication skills, and multiple educational leadership topics. Her greatest honors include serving as the first president and executive director of the Texas Staff Development Council and serving as board member and president of the National Staff Development Council (now Learning Forward) from 1994–1999. Kathy is a founding member of Coaching For Results Global and serves as one of its board directors, responsible for the Teaching and Learning Division.

**Sue Kidd, MS,** is a leadership coach trained and certified by Coaching For Results Global, with six years' experience coaching school leaders. She is the coordinator for the Kansas Partnership in Character Education grant and has served as president of the Kansas Staff Development Council and of the Kansas Gifted, Talented, and Creative Association. Sue has been honored as a nominee for the Kansas Teacher of the Year and the Kansas Master Teacher.

**Riva Korashan, MEd, ACC,** was a founding member of Coaching For Results Global and passionately believed that coaching educators is the key to student achievement. In her work as a program coordinator for the United Federation of Teachers' Teacher Center, Riva coached her colleagues to deliver the highest quality professional learning in their work as school-based coaches and school-improvement specialists. She was one of twenty-seven staff developers nationally to be chosen by the National Staff Development Council (now Learning Forward) to be trained by the Brande Foundation to provide life coaching to school administrators of high-poverty schools and school districts in order to improve student learning. Riva's passion and love will remain forever in our hearts.

**Gina Marx, EdD,** is currently an assistant professor in the Newman University School of Education Graduate Department and works with aspiring principals in the Building Leadership Program. She is also one of eight Kansas leadership coaches for Coaching For Results Global and a Kansas Learning Network implementation coach for schools on improvement. Gina has been in education twenty-six years, serving as an assistant superintendent, staff development director and grant writer for a thirty-three district consortium, high school principal, assistant high school principal, middle school at-risk coordinator, secondary communications/English/ESL instructor. She also served as vice-president of United School Administrators, president of Kansas ASCD, and is currently the higher education representative for Learning Forward Kansas.

**Dayna Richardson, MEd,** has served as an assistant superintendent, a teacher and coordinator of gifted education, and the original director of an educational service center in Kansas, and is also one of eight Kansas coaches for Coaching For Results Global. She has worked extensively with professional learning communities, including Adaptive Schools, data driven dialogue, and teacher leadership. Dayna was Staff Developer of the Year for the group now known as Learning Forward Kansas, and she has been awarded the Kansas ASCD Outstanding Curriculum Leader.

**Reba Schumacher, MEd, PCC,** is a veteran Texas public school administrator with thirty-three years' experience including service as an executive director, supervisor of principals, and principal. Reba has coached numerous educators from large urban inner city school districts to small rural districts across the United States and continues to coach high-achieving, goal-driven individuals wishing to bring value and excellence to their organizations. In addition to individual coaching, she is a seminar facilitator for Coaching For Results Global and has provided professional development to hundreds of educators in large and small districts as well as for regional educational service centers.

**Frances Shuster, MEd, PCC,** a coauthor of *RESULTS Coaching* (Corwin, 2010) has been coaching for over ten years in the areas of leadership development, transformational change, executive effectiveness, and strategic thinking and planning. She is a founding member and president of the nonprofit organization, Coaching For Results

Global, an active member of the International Coach Federation (ICF), 2006 president of the International Coach Federation, North Texas Chapter, and credentialed as a PCC. She is a faculty member and coach in the University of Texas at Dallas School of Management, and is an international presenter and expert facilitator.

**Diana Williams, PhD, PCC,** has been an urban educator for over thirty years, serving as principal, staff development supervisor, central office administrator for a parent/community involvement initiative, resource teacher, classroom teacher, and a university program coordinator. She is the lead author of *The Elementary Principal's Personal Coach* (Corwin, 2010), as well as numerous articles. Diana was a member of the board of trustees for the National Staff Development Council (now Learning Forward) for six years and served as president of the board in 1994. She was cofounder and past president of the Staff Development Council of Ohio, was on the Phi Delta Kappa board in Columbus, Ohio, and currently is on the board of Coaching For Results Global.

**David Winans, EdD, PCC,** for over thirty-eight years has maintained a constant commitment to serving community through ever improving learning: as a teacher of learners ages six to sixty, as a leader of private and public educational systems, as a collaborator involved with the founding of seven associations that still fulfill the niche each was created to serve, and as a life coach to leaders answering their own calling. Dale Carnegie's observation that success is having what you want and happiness is wanting what you have both powers and integrates Dave personally and professionally.

*To Riva, for encouraging us to always dance!*

*To our coaching clients who provide wonderful examples of coach-leader behaviors and inspire us each day with their commitment and desire to make schools great places for ALL children.*

# What Is a Coaching Conversation?

*The conversation is the relationship.*

—Susan Scott, *Fierce Conversations*

Imagine you have just visited a classroom where the teacher is presenting the best math lesson you have ever observed. The room is attractively decorated with stimulating resources and learning centers. Students are actively engaged with each other as they test their hypotheses about why some of their math problems have more than one correct answer. The teacher has placed her pupils in groups differentiated by their skills and learning styles. She moves from table to table, asking the students to explain their analyses of the problems and the conclusions they have drawn. Their responses demonstrate a deep understanding of both the problem-solving processes and mathematical concepts involved. When the bell rings signaling the end of the period, the children reluctantly put away their materials and linger to discuss their thinking in more depth with the teacher.

You leave the classroom exhilarated and excited by what you have just observed, and you are looking forward to discussing the lesson with the teacher and providing her with feedback.

Let's examine two different conversations you might have with the math teacher.

## Conversation 1

Observer:    I really enjoyed observing your fourth period math class today. You definitely know how to keep your students engaged in the lesson. They seemed to have a lot of fun, yet they also understood the math concepts you had taught them. It's amazing how you even differentiated their instruction. I was as sorry to see the class end as your pupils were. In fact, I think that was the best lesson I have ever seen taught in our school. I know if I were your supervisor, I would be giving you an outstanding rating for that lesson.

Math teacher:    Thanks for visiting my class and for your kind compliments. Come back any time.

## Conversation 2

Observer:    That was an amazing math lesson you taught to your fourth period math class today. You clearly emphasized higher order thinking skills that caused them to reflect deeply about their hypotheses rather than just have them practice a page of problems. I am interested in trying a similar approach in social studies and wonder what steps you took to get your students to this level of thinking.

Math teacher:    As I plan my lessons, I always think about ways to engage students in reflective thinking rather than just parroting back to me a bunch of memorized information. Last year, I decided to focus on asking my classes open-ended questions rather than ones that had just a one-word answer. I emphasized that I wanted their best thinking and that there were many possible answers to my questions. I utilized this technique for at least ten minutes in every class.

Observer:    What else did you do?

Math teacher:    I knew I also wanted students to be active learners and to begin to differentiate their instruction. That's when I decided to place the students in small, but flexible work groups. I also encouraged them to help one another to think about and solve problems together rather than compete against each other.

**Observer:** But how do you grade the students if they are helping each other and working together?

**Math teacher:** That was originally a dilemma for me. Then I had a discussion with the principal about an alternative assessment process. Instead of giving the typical numerical or letter grades, the principal gave me permission to develop rubrics for each set of skills and to provide students and parents with feedback about where individual students were on the rubric scale as they moved toward mastery of the content.

**Observer:** Wow! That sounds like a lot of extra work. How did you get the support of students and parents for this new rating process?

**Math teacher:** It was difficult at first, until I refined the rubrics and the students and parents learned and became accustomed to the new rating process. While it takes more thought on my part, you observed how engaged the students are in their learning. And because they are really thinking about the content, students understand concepts more quickly. They are actually working about four weeks ahead of students in the traditional math classes in this school! Moreover, they performed exceptionally well on the state math test last March, and I never hear my students say "I hate math."

**Observer:** I am really anxious to begin a similar teaching process in my social studies classes. Over the weekend, I plan to think about and sketch out some lessons to teach later next week. What would you be willing to do to provide me with some feedback about my plans and ideas?

**Math teacher:** I would be happy to meet with you during our common planning time on Monday.

**Observer:** Thanks! I'll see you on Monday.

What do you notice about the two different conversations? Which conversation would you prefer to participate in? The first conversation was typical of the kind of feedback excellent teachers receive, with some statements about how good their teaching is. Average and marginal teachers often receive similar feedback except they also receive a long list of recommended changes for improvement in addition to a couple of statements about the lesson.

The first "conversation" was not really a conversation at all. A conversation implies that at least two people are talking with and listening to each other. In addition, the first example provided the math teacher with positive, yet very vague feedback about her teaching. Consequently, the observer's remarks provided no clues as to what teaching skills she should continue to reinforce and what processes she might wish to modify for her students. The social studies teacher knew he had observed exemplary practices, yet he had little insight as to how he, too, could develop such excellent lessons.

The second conversation included a number of coach-like behaviors on the part of the social studies teacher, including committed listening, paraphrasing, powerful speaking and open-ended questions, and reflective feedback. The observer really paid attention to the teacher and students during the class period and he listened fully as the math teacher described her thinking and processes for developing her lesson plans. Instead of asking questions that could be answered with a one-word response, such as, "Did it take you a lot of time to plan your lessons?" the observer asked several open-ended questions that provided the math teacher with an opportunity to reflect on her thinking and to share relevant information. For example, when the issue of grading came up, the math teacher explained in detail how she solved that dilemma. Instead of just saying that the teacher's lesson was great, the observer provided her with very specific feedback, stating that she "clearly emphasized higher order thinking skills that caused them [students] to reflect deeply about their hypotheses rather than just have them practice a page of problems." This reflective and specific feedback cued the math teacher that her efforts were on the right track and that she would want to continue such practices in the future. Her students did not just enjoy math class, they actually engaged in the higher order thinking skills that the teacher wanted them to practice.

The second conversation was a true dialogue between the math and social studies teachers. The math teacher benefitted from the opportunity to reflect on her practices, and the social studies teacher gained insight into how he might implement similar exemplary practices with the guidance of his colleague.

## DEFINING A COACHING CONVERSATION

Not all conversations are coaching conversations. First, a coach-like conversation is very intentional and often includes prethought. Second, a coaching conversation focuses on the other person, his strengths and challenges, and the attributes he brings to the conversation. Third, the purpose of coaching conversations is to stimulate thinking, growth, and change that lead to action.

> The purpose of coaching conversations is to stimulate thinking, growth, and change that lead to action.

Of course school personnel already engage in many types of conversations such as supervisory conferences and mentoring sessions. Teachers engage in joint planning discussions and often have interactions that are just friendly dialogues.

Twenty-first century schools require collaboration and clear communication among all of the school's constituents. Coach-leaders "believe in others' ability to grow and excel. They communicate through their coaching conversations that they see themselves as partners—not bosses" (Cheliotes & Reilly, 2010, p. 15). Recent brain research (Rock, 2006) demonstrates that motivating self and others to change requires transforming our long-established brain patterns. The deep reflection fostered by coaching conversations enables us to create and deepen new neural pathways in the brain. Through coaching conversations, both parties leave the dialogue feeling competent and confident in themselves and appreciative of the support from the other person.

Sometimes you may find it difficult to hold certain conversations for fear that you will harm a relationship, cause anger, or that your words will be unproductive. However, true coaching conversations open the space for yourself and others to reflect deeply, understand each other's viewpoints, and provide feedback that does not attack an individual, but rather, creates room for personal choice and productive action. The more you practice being intentional and invitational in your conversations, the more often you will experience positive results from your dialogues with others.

Next, we will examine several very specific, essential coach-like skills that you will be able to incorporate into your daily conversations. We recommend that you practice these skills first with a trusted colleague, friend, or family member until you are comfortable integrating the skills into your daily interactions. We also recommend that you consult our prior book, *Coaching Conversations: Transforming Your School One Conversation at a Time* (Cheliotes & Reilly, 2010) for more in-depth discussion and practice of the fundamental skills employed in coaching conversations.

## THE FOUR ESSENTIAL SKILLS FOR HOLDING COACHING CONVERSATIONS

### Committed Listening

Committed listening connects you powerfully with others because you intentionally focus on the other person. Your full attention conveys that you value the speaker and that you sincerely want to engage in a dialogue rather than a monologue. Committed listening helps build trust relationships. In fact, committed listening is foundational to all coaching conversations.

> When you are a committed listener, you pay close attention to both the verbal and nonverbal cues of the person speaking.

When you are a committed listener, you pay close attention to both the verbal and nonverbal cues of the person speaking. For example, if a colleague shares that he is happy about working on the district's new data committee, yet his facial expression and tone of voice convey otherwise, he has given you important nonverbal cues about his real feelings. At that point you might respond, "You have said that you are excited about being on the data committee, yet your voice and facial expression seem sad. I am wondering what you are really thinking about your new assignment?" Then the other person may choose to share his real feelings because you have provided a space for him to do so. As a committed listener, you would be silent as the speaker reflects on your question. Because you are being a committed listener, you would avoid giving your colleague advice, stating how you feel about the situation, eschew judging his decision, and keep quiet about what you have done in similar situations. You would just listen and encourage deep reflection in your colleague by paraphrasing his statements.

## Paraphrasing

The second essential skill in coaching conversations is paraphrasing. Paraphrasing is a shorthand statement or summary of what another person tells you. It helps the speaker clarify his thinking and aligns the thinking of both the speaker and listener. In the example above, when you said,

> Paraphrasing helps the speaker clarify his thinking and aligns the thinking of both the speaker and listener.

"You seem sad," the speaker might have responded, "Yes, I really am feeling down about this extra assignment." On the other hand, he also might have stated another feeling, such as, "Actually, I am feeling more angry than sad about this appointment because it will take valuable time away from my family activities." Now you have a clearer picture of his thinking and are better able to hold a productive conversation with him. At the same time, by listening to him and paraphrasing his statements without giving advice or interrupting him with your own judgment or story, you have deepened the level of trust between you.

Paraphrasing sends the message that you are fully listening, care about what he is saying, and understand, or are trying to understand, his point of view.

## Presuming Positive Intent and Asking Powerful Questions

The third essential set of skills in coaching conversations is presuming positive intent about the other person and asking powerful, open-ended questions. Our language is filled with negativity. *You are wrong. That is incorrect. Why don't you think before you act? You must be mistaken. How could you possibly say that?* In fact, from his own anecdotal research, David Rock (2006, p. 59) estimates that the average person engages in thousands of hours of self-criticism each year as well as countless hours of perceived criticism from others. In addition, he found that most people receive positive feedback a total of *three minutes* on average per year. These are astounding statistics! Is it any wonder that many of us are afraid to take risks, change our behaviors, or trust our self and others?

> Presuming positive intent means that we enter into a conversation with a positive mindset about the other person and our language conveys this positivity to the individual.

Presuming positive intent is a totally new frame of thinking for many of us. Presuming positive intent means that we enter into a conversation with a positive mindset about the other person and our language conveys this positivity to the individual. For example, a principal may begin a conversation with a teacher with the words, "Because you are someone who wants your students to excel in reading comprehension, what objectives have you written for this week's language arts lessons that will emphasize their understanding of character development in the novels your class is reading?" This statement demonstrates a positive view of the other person by presuming a positive intention on the part of the teacher—that she is dedicated to having her students excel in reading comprehension. Moreover, the teacher has now been invited to share her ideas for teaching her students about character development. Again, by presuming a positive intention on the part of the teacher and by asking an open-ended question, the supervisor has provided a place for reflection, true dialogue, and development of trust.

In contrast, supervisory personnel often speak with teachers by asking, "Do you have any objectives for your lesson?" This statement presumes that the teacher has no objectives for her lesson and has a high probability of building a barrier between the teacher and supervisor. Moreover, by asking a close-ended question that can only be answered *yes* or *no*, there is no motivation for the teacher to reflect or share her thoughts with the supervisor. In addition, the trust relationship between the supervisor and teacher may deteriorate because of this negative approach.

At this point, you may be wondering how presuming positive intent may be used with someone who typically does not carry through on his responsibilities. The solution is still to make a positive presupposition about the individual. In other words, you would still take a positive approach by asking, "What objectives have you developed for the lesson?" The teacher may be a bit disconcerted at first by this positive inquiry, yet if you consistently make positive presuppositions about the person by asking him positive, open-ended questions, you are actually challenging him to grow and change within a safe space. He will eventually truly reflect on his lesson development and how his teaching processes affect students.

In their book, *Appreciative Coaching,* Orem, Binkert, and Clancy (2007) write the following:

> Appreciative jolts are immediate experiences of attention, valuing, and affirmation that cause the person to change his self-expectations, bring up positive emotion, and move to a more positive self-image—all of which can lead the person to positive action. (pp. 52–53)

By taking a positive approach with difficult people, you have much to gain and nothing to lose. You have the opportunity to build trust and collaboration, improve the self-esteem of others, and provide a safe space for growth and change. The message you send when you speak powerfully through positive presuppositions and asking open-ended questions is, "I trust you, I support you, and it is okay to take risks."

## Reflective Feedback

Reflective feedback is the fourth essential coaching conversation skill. We all need feedback to grow, to learn, and to understand the path we are following. In education, we are always giving feedback. Teachers tell students about their progress, principals give teachers feedback about their instructional practices and student achievement, and superintendents give feedback to principals about the success of their schools.

Much of the feedback given is judgmental:

- You are doing a good job.
- I think you should try . . . .
- Here are my concerns.

David Perkins, the author of *King Arthur's Round Table: How Collaborative Conversations Create Smart Organizations* (2003), says there is both good news and bad news about feedback. "The good news is that feedback is essential for individual, community, and organizational effectiveness and learning. The bad news is that feedback often flops, yielding no meaningful exchange of information and driving people apart" (p. 42).

Imagine you are an assistant principal and the principal tells you that the new language arts instructional program you have been diligently working on with the third-grade teachers is a waste of time. The students don't seem to be achieving any better and the teachers are complaining about the extra work involved. How would you feel? Angry, defeated, alienated, undermined? In the principal's mind, she had a duty to be upfront and direct with you, yet that is of no help to you. While it is essential for you to know what is or is not working, this direct negative feedback has not helped you grow as an instructional leader. Moreover, you now are less motivated to try new ideas in the future and your trust relationship with the principal has diminished. Lay-it-on-the-line negative criticism is not the kind of feedback that helps you grow professionally or personally.

Now let's turn this scenario around. The principal has some serious doubts about the effectiveness of your work with the third-grade teachers, but she really likes you and does not want to hurt your feelings or her relationship with you. So, instead of being directly critical of you, her feedback is vague. She tells you that the project you have been working on is "interesting" and a "good effort." She then states, "You might want to talk with the teachers about how they feel about the new process. I'm sure everything will work out fine." You leave the conversation feeling positive at first and then begin to wonder what the principal was really saying to you. What is a "good effort" and what was she implying when she mentioned that you should talk with the teachers? The principal's conciliatory feedback has, on the surface, left you feeling fine, yet at the same time, you have a nagging suspicion that something is wrong. Because the principal's comments were so vague, you have received no direct feedback about the new third-grade initiative and feel unsure about your next steps. While the principal's conciliatory feedback has preserved your relationship with her, you still do not have sufficient specific feedback to grow and learn.

Coaching For Results Global teaches coach-leaders a third type of feedback called reflective feedback in *Coaching Strategies for Powerful Leading* (2011, adapted from Perkins, 2003). The objective in reflective feedback is to give honest and direct comments while at the same time preserving relationships. There are three steps to

> The objective in reflective feedback is to give honest and direct comments while at the same time preserving relationships.

this process that may require more prethought than typical feedback conversations, yet also are very intentional on the part of the speaker.

Step 1 focuses on asking clarifying questions so that it is clear to both parties what the idea or behavior under consideration is. In the conversation with the assistant principal, the principal might have asked, "In what ways do you see the new third-grade language arts instructional process different from what the teachers were doing before?" Another question might be, "How have the students responded to the new program? In other words, what data have you gathered that supports continued use of this new approach?"

The second step of reflective feedback specifically expresses the value or value potential of the idea or behavior. For example, the principal might say, "You have really put in a lot of time researching this new instructional program and sharing this information with the teachers." She might also have stated, "While visiting the third-grade classrooms I have seen specific evidence that the teachers are implementing the program. Their rooms are filled with student work containing very relevant comments by the teachers to the students about their thinking processes."

The third part of reflective feedback poses reflective questions or possibilities. For example, the principal might ask the assistant principal, "How are you aligning the new instructional system with the core curriculum content standards?" She might also say, "I have had some comments from the teachers about the amount of time the new program takes to plan lessons in accordance with the directions provided. I wonder what modifications the third-grade teachers might make to the program so that their personal teaching styles would be reflected in their lessons and they would be more accepting of the new process?"

As you see, reflective feedback is very specific. Both parties in the conversation are clear about what is being discussed, the relationship between them is preserved because there is a place for honest dialogue to take place, and both people have opportunities to reflect on the process without becoming defensive, argumentative, or evasive.

Now let's look at how one school leader applied the four essential coaching skills to become a true coach-leader for his school district.

## Coach-Leader Man—Feeding the Hunger!

### Vicky Dearing

Dave was a man with a passion growing from within. He was a school leader hungry for a new way of leading! He was just like you or me. He looked out across his school district—somewhere in the USA—and thought, "Why not here and why not now!" And, thus began Dave's amazing journey toward becoming an authentic Coach-Leader—a title with which he was not yet familiar. Dave did his homework. He investigated. He realized that to increase student results in his district, he would be called to motivate and challenge others to increase their own thinking.

And so Dave began to learn coach-like behaviors. He took coach-specific seminars and included other key players in his district so that together they were creating a collaborative culture of new ways of talking, thinking, and being, both as individuals and as a team. Together this district team of educators learned new skills for actually listening to what others were saying, without the need to interrupt, promote their own conclusions, or solve issues for the speaker. They learned how to move to a state of curiosity and wonderment. They learned language that supports others to think in free flowing and clearer ways. They learned how to be solution-focused thinking partners rather than wallowing together in the problems. In addition, they learned that this new way of being and doing had the potential to actually accelerate results. They also worked individually with a leadership coach, over a continuous span of time, which elevated their understanding about the impact of being coach-like in leading others.

So, what difference has this passion and hunger made in the life of Dave and his district? The journey's not over and yet it is making a big difference in the way thinking is done in the district. Being a coach-leader is taking hold in his district. Dave is well on his way to having every administrator, including the superintendent, and every instructional coach, both at the district and school level, trained in coach-like behaviors. Today, school colleagues are actually holding authentic conversations using a Professional Learning Community (PLC) protocol, and school leaders are showing up as coach-leaders as they interact with staff, parents, students, and the community. Today, Dave's district has created a clearer vision for the future with a firm commitment for stronger results for all students.

Hunger cries out for nourishment. When that hunger is for changes in the way we lead schools, there is no better way to feed that hunger than by feeding the coach-leader that's living inside each of us. That's what happened for Dave and it can happen for you!

## Coaching Insights

Dave's story illustrates how one person dedicated to becoming a coach-leader was able to affect the culture of his entire district. Through coach-specific training, individual coaching, and communication among the district's administrators about their goals and values, Dave and his colleagues are well on their way to creating a districtwide culture in which every member is coach-like in their thinking, state of being, and actions.

## FINAL THOUGHTS

At the end of each chapter you will have an opportunity to review the key concepts in that chapter. You will also have a place to journal your own ideas about coaching conversations—the skills you want to utilize and how you want to be in your coach-leader conversations. The stories in the book provide you with successful coaching conversations others have used. However, the real value in this book is what you decide to do with the information, skills, and exemplars as you apply *Opening the Door to Coaching Conversations*.

---

### Key Skills for Coaching Conversations

- Listen with commitment.
  - Focus on the other person.
  - Invite reflection and dialogue.
  - Be nonjudgmental.
  - Include times of silence.
  - Avoid advice giving.
- Paraphrase what the other person says.
- Presume positive intent and utilize powerful, open-ended questions.
- Communicate using reflective feedback.
  - Clarify for understanding.
  - Express the value or value potential of an idea or behavior.
  - Pose reflective questions or possibilities.

---

Use the space on page 15 to describe your ideal self and school. How might you use the four essential coaching skills to make your ideal self and school a reality?

## Your Learning

1. How will you use coaching conversations in your daily life?

2. Which of the four essential coach-leader skills will you practice first and with whom will you practice?

3. What is the "state of being" you would like to present to others as you have coaching conversations with them?

4. How will you know when you are holding effective coaching conversations?

_____

_____

_____

_____

_____

_____

_____

_____

_____

_____

_____

_____

_____

_____

_____

_____

_____

# Discovering and Using
# Your Core Values

*Teamwork is almost always lacking within organizations
that fail, and often present within those that succeed*

—Patrick Lencioni, *Overcoming the Five
Dysfunctions of a Team*

A very frustrating occurrence for leaders is when a team they depend upon begins to fall apart. The "complaint-of-the-day" becomes a smoke screen for general discontent, malaise, and frustration. Team members may resort to passive-aggressive behavior during the meetings and hold "parking lot conversations" about their discontent that infects others after the meetings. Team members do not attend meetings and are not doing their promised work between meetings. They are overly argumentative and nitpicky about details that don't seem to matter. Internal strife and disrespect is evident. Everyone on the team feels on edge and stressed. Morale is low.

In his book, *Overcoming the Five Dysfunctions of a Team: A Field Guide for Leaders, Managers, and Facilitator*, Patrick Lencioni (2005) makes the case that well-functioning teams are critical to getting good results. He says, "in this day and age of informational ubiquity and nanosecond change, teamwork remains the one sustainable competitive advantage" (p. 3).

Lencioni (2002) observes that in strong teams, members trust each other. They engage in "unfiltered conflict around ideas" (p. 189). They commit to decisions and plans of action, hold each other accountable for delivering those plans, and focus on achievement of *team* results.

Lencioni also believes that working in well-functioning teams is fulfilling. This sounds a lot like the concept of "purpose" in Daniel Pink's 2009 book, *Drive: The Surprising Truth About What Motivates Us*. Pink explains, "Humans by their nature seek purpose—a cause greater and more enduring than themselves" (p. 208).

In well-functioning teams, people come together and set aside their individual needs for the good of the whole. This satisfies their search for purpose and brings them feelings of satisfaction and fulfillment.

Pink identifies three important factors in motivating people: autonomy, mastery, and purpose. When people have input and options, when their work challenges them to hone their skills, and when they have a clear and meaningful purpose, they become engaged and productive members within their relationships. Discontent and cynicism are often merely symptoms that a person has lost sight of meaning and purpose for involvement.

> Coaching conversations about core values help people reconnect to what their common hopes and dreams are.

We have many teams in school systems: professional learning communities, content departments, principal groups, superintendent cabinets, school boards, and so on. When a team seems to be falling apart, it is time to begin conversations about core values, common vision, and purpose. Such conversations help people reconnect to what their hopes and dreams once were. Spotlighting core values raises the plane of the conversation for the team—from the messiness of the current complaint to "What do we believe *in common?*" and "Why are we here in the first place?" These kinds of coaching conversations invite people to talk about what they want from the group that they are not getting. Lencioni (2005) agrees that " this sense of common cause and unification often has a powerful effect on everyone" (p. 58).

Clint's story is a good example of how a conversation about priorities helped move the school board forward in gaining clarity about what was most important about their decisions.

## From Terminator to Hope Builder

### Marceta Fleming Reilly

Clint had been the "terminator" the previous year as superintendent. He had made many very tough, courageous decisions about closing schools and reassigning staff or reducing positions. This year he was determined to be a "hope builder" for the district. The district no longer needed to worry so much about the budget, and he was determined to create a family-like school district where everyone cared for and supported each other.

But Clint had a problem with his school board. Three new members had been elected recently and one of them was always harping about high taxes. This board member was lobbying to make cutbacks in every line item even though the district had just completed painful school closings in order to bring the budget back to a sustainable level.

Clint was very frustrated because morale was already low among staff members due to all the changes in the previous year, and what they needed was recognition and respect—not more haranguing about benefits costing too much or overuse of paper products!

Clint regularly held board work sessions before each of the monthly board meetings. At one of these sessions he asked, "When the school year is over, what do you want the community to be saying about the actions of the board?" Individually board members named things like honesty, forthrightness, valuing taxpayers' dollars, and doing good things for kids.

Then he asked, "What can we say we want *collectively* as a board for our community?" Board members had some deep discussion about this and finally agreed that they wanted "a top-notch school at a reasonable cost."

Clint liked the sound of that, so at the next work session he asked, "Who are our stakeholders in helping us provide the community with a top-notch school at a reasonable cost?" Here the board members listed staff, students, parents, school and community leaders, and taxpayers.

Next, he asked the board members to collectively prioritize these stakeholder groups as to their importance in developing and maintaining a "top-notch school at a reasonable cost." Naturally, *staff* and *students* were high on the list and *taxpayer*, though important, was lower.

*(Continued)*

(Continued)

By working with his board to clarify their collective vision and goals for their work, Clint was able to put cost-cutting issues in perspective for the board team. They realized that keeping an eye on the budget is important, but they also had to attend to the legitimate needs of staff members and students in order to create and maintain a top-notch school.

## Coaching Insights

Clint trusted that the members of the school board had the best interests of the community in mind as they worked. He wanted them to speak from the heart about values that mattered to them individually because he knew that would draw out their best selves.

He asked open-ended, provocative questions that sparked thinking. Through good listening, Clint was able to identify themes that emerged from the board discussions. He helped them highlight similarities and identify collective consensus on ideas.

In subsequent board meetings Clint used their language to make connections from the current tasks to their collective values and goals. This continued the glow from the original meeting and helped them become intentional about aligning their work with their common goals. As the board developed their sense of connection to meaningful purpose for their work, they began to function better as a team. They had greater trust, richer discussions, and better attention to true priorities.

In the next story, a new principal has a burning goal for his school and learns how to transmit his passion to the staff by getting clear about his core values.

## A Yearning for More

### Karen Anderson

Imagine a school where every classroom teacher believes that math is more about *thinking* than *doing calculations*. This *IS* the goal of a New Jersey principal who wants to transform his school into such a thinking place.

Mark wants strong planning for high-quality math lessons that offer clarity about what students will know and be able to do rather than activities or processes that teachers use to teach a specific skill. He wants to observe rich conversations about the multiple strategies students are using to solve problems. And, he wants to see high levels of success in mathematics.

Interestingly enough, Mark knows this change begins with him. In order to increase the capacity of staff members and students, he must first increase his own capacity to think mathematically—he wants to work on his own mindset. He wants to "hold up" the standards and expectations in both his *being* and his *doing*. Toward that end, he wants to be a learner, to pay attention to the questions he asks, and to make sure he speaks about the outcomes of what he wants to learn over the activities he will do to learn. In other words, he wants to be a coach-leader who models what he wants teachers to be doing with their students. He intends to make math his focus when he visits the classrooms in his school, in the lesson planning his teachers complete, and in the conversations he creates in his faculty meetings. He wants to ask mediating questions that build thinking capacity in his staff and ultimately his students.

This goal emerged through conversations with his coach as he spoke about next steps for his school. Admittedly, while student performance looked pretty good on paper, Mark wanted more for his students. With the space and time to conceptualize and build the detail and description of how he could take his school to the next level of learning, his vision unfolded. Using a combination of the coach-leader behaviors of committed listening and reflective questions with his staff, he began to fill in the gaps for moving his school forward, with him being at the center of that change.

This principal had a gnawing, a yearning for more for his students mathematically in spite of what performance assessments indicated. He knew there was untapped potential bubbling just below the surface. He used the mantra "Math is more about thinking than doing!" as his inspiration to create a plan to support his dreams for his students—one that would unleash the potential and take his school to greater heights.

## Coaching Insights

This principal began by looking at himself before he worked with others. He became very intentional about how he wanted to "show up" for others. Despite that tests of performance said everything was

OK, he believed his students could do better so he wanted more for them. He practiced committed listening in order to *hear* himself and others through conversations. He got clarity around his vision for what he wanted for his school in terms of math—what it looked like and sounded like when actualized. Then he held up the standards and expectations of his vision to others. He worked hard to show congruency between what he said was important and what he did on a daily basis. He used reflective questions to promote and provoke the thinking of others. By engaging in these kinds of conversations, Mark built trust, support, and commitment for the vision. He had transformed it from *his* vision, to *their* vision, to a vision for the school—a *collective and shared* vision!

The next story is about a new principal who wanted to change a "sacred tradition" at the school. Her core values and purpose become the firm foundation for initiating the change.

## Courage at the Core

### Riva Korashan

It takes great courage for a first-year principal to change a cherished school tradition, and that is exactly the work that Alice has done this year.

The long-standing tradition at Alice's school has been to hold an annual Halloween parade where students dressed in their favorite costumes followed by individual classroom parties. But things have changed over the years. Data showed that about 14–15% of the parents wanted to opt their children out of what is supposed to be a schoolwide celebration. The school's population has grown over the years, and the physical space could no longer safely accommodate all the students, parents, and siblings who attend the parade. At this year's celebration, it was difficult to monitor who was in the building, and all the cars in the parking lot created safety concerns. There was no space to hold an alternative activity for those students who were not participating in the parade. Staff members came to Alice after the event and expressed their desire to do something different to celebrate Halloween next year. But would attempting to change this tradition cause divisions within the school and conflict with parents? Was this something that Alice wanted to take on her first year as principal? Was there the possibility that a small group of parents might use this issue to push their own political agenda of "maintaining American values"?

Alice and her coach used their coaching conversations to explore this issue. To help Alice clarify her core values, she reflected on what she wanted the purpose of this event to be. Without missing a beat, she was able to articulate that she wanted all the students in the school to be able to participate in a safe, fun celebration that is meaningfully connected to instruction and can be easily managed during school time. That clarity gave Alice the courage to proceed.

She also asked herself, "What opportunity does this present for my growth as principal?" This helped Alice create several reframes for the issue. She moved from her fears of possibly alienating parents to focusing on creating opportunities to strengthen relationships with them. Knowing she needed support from her staff to pursue this change, she saw an opportunity to ask her school leadership team for their support and involvement. Together they crafted talking points about the Halloween celebration to present at a PTA meeting and include in a school newsletter sent to all parents. Alice realized that this was an opportunity to deliver a strong message about her leadership beliefs and style. Her belief in collaboration became evident in her work with the PTA as well as the school leadership team. Alice now has a parent-teacher committee working on creating a new fall celebration for next year.

Clarifying her goals and purpose gave Alice the greatest gift of all—the confidence that moving forward on changing this tradition was the right thing to do and in the best interests for all the students in her school. Changing this one tradition laid the foundation for staff and community to have a mechanism to express their shared values. This new collaboration was possible because Alice took the courageous step of examining and sharing her core values.

## Coaching Insights

In the beginning, Alice was intimidated by the idea of taking on a deeply established school tradition in her first year as principal. She knew her success was rooted in how well she established trust and rapport with staff members and community. Yet when she considered her own core values, she knew this was an issue she had to face.

To start, she got very clear about the purpose she saw for the event and what she wanted. Then she thought about how she wanted to be perceived as a leader as she worked with staff and community to initiate the change.

She used several reframes to help her approach the change task with positive intent:

- From "alienating parents" to engaging them
- From "fighting with the staff" to involving them
- From "being the boss" to having an opportunity to collaborate with staff and community

In the end, Alice discovered that this issue was the perfect platform for her to introduce her vision and values to the school and demonstrate what kind of leader she wanted to be.

The final story is about a newly appointed principal who is saddled with an assistant principal with no experience. She uses her core values to frame how she works with him, and it makes all the difference.

## Leading With Your Core Values

### Dave Winans

He was young to be an assistant principal, but had demonstrated great gifts in the classroom; he was thoughtful, intelligent, bursting with energy and dedication. The veteran principal, new to the building, understood why her predecessor would promote someone with so much potential. Yet the students and staff had great needs. The principal and the school would endure significant negative consequences without clear, positive achievement. How she handled this new, young "pup" as her coadministrator was the first critical decision in leading the troubled school to high performance.

The principal's analysis came down to these options:

- She could insist that the superintendent allow her to select a different, more experienced assistant.

- She could mentor the young administrator, telling him what he should do, when he should do it, and how long he should continue.
- She could coach the young administrator, following her beliefs about how to facilitate learning and results.

She aligned her first critical decision with the kind of learning place that she wanted the school to become. She wanted unshakable commitment to each learner's worth and to professionals' ability to integrate and accurately evaluate multiple sources of information. She desired a creative partnership among learners and leaders, upholding a balance between individual learning aspirations and system learning requirements. She knew that a structure for sustained progress toward achievement would be imperative. Finally, she wanted a learning place that would be focused on results and open to multiple paths for achieving them.

The new principal chose to coach and it made all the difference. Over time, the young administrator, the members of the staff, and the students appreciated her commitment to facilitating learning and results. She helped create awareness of needed changes, and then together, they designed actions, planned and set goals, and monitored progress for accountability.

The attributes for the learning place she wanted were honed out of the practices of successful leaders and the research of effective learning. There is nothing easy or natural about adhering to these coach-leader attributes. There is less immediate gratification to the coach compared to someone who is the "sage-on-the-stage." There is significant pressure from learners who do not want to be accountable for their own learning and from critics who want "command" to be all that is necessary. Spending time in meaningful conversations to build trust and the capacity of others can be a hard sell in this age of instant gratification and whizbang technology.

The veteran principal new to the building chose to coach. In so doing, she aligned herself for the time when she would be a retired principal at the pinnacle of her career. She would have the deep satisfaction that her successor would be leading a school whose culture exuded the attributes for facilitating true learning and results.

## Coaching Insights

This principal knew she needed to walk her talk if she was going to establish trust and rapport in this challenging school. She was very clear about her core values and what she wanted in the school. She used coaching conversations as opportunities to hold up these standards and expectations, and she involved staff members in designing what they would look and sound like in classroom instruction. She treated her staff as she wanted them to treat the students. Together they created ways to meaningfully monitor student learning and adjust instruction for maximum results.

By believing in the leadership potential of the young assistant principal, she was communicating to her staff that *they* too had the capacity to significantly improve student results. She drew out the best work from staff members by connecting them to big meaningful goals and inviting them to become the change they wanted to see.

---

### Key Ideas for Discovering and Using Core Values

- Presume the positive intent of others.
- Identify and acknowledge the strengths and value potential of others.
- Ask thought-provoking questions that assist others in thinking about ideas greater than daily minutia.
  - This is thinking from a "balcony view" or thinking about the "bigger game."
- Help others identify what they want as a result of their work.
- Probe for specificity:
  - Challenge contradictions.
  - Help identify key points of agreement and disagreement.
- Use the common values and goals that emerge as standards and expectations to inform decisions and to measure impact.
- Make connections between common values/vision, and the current work being done.

## Your Learning

1. What in these stories resonates with you? Why?

2. What are the core values with which you wish to lead?

3. How are you thinking about sharing these values with your team?

_____

_____

_____

_____

_____

_____

_____

_____

_____

_____

_____

_____

_____

_____

_____

_____

_____

# Building Trust and
# Community

*The essential insight is that people will be accountable
and committed to what they have a hand in creating.*

—Peter Block, *Community: The Structure of Belonging*

**B**uilding trust and an appreciation of community within a school
setting are essential components for holding authentic, reflective
conversations. Trust and a sense of community among stakeholders
are also important factors in creating an environment within which
change and continuous learning may occur. In *Schools That Learn*
(Senge et al., 2000), Peter Senge notes the following:

> Healthy professional communities are safe places in
> which to examine practices, try new ideas, and acknowl-
> edge mistakes. . . . Strong professional community doesn't
> just happen. It requires delib-
> erate attention by leaders
> across the system. Indeed, the
> single most strategic thing
> that school leaders can do is to

> Trust building is integral to
> relationship building.

create conditions that foster professional community—a culture of interaction and reflective dialogue. (p. 328)

Trust requires openness to others, honesty, consistency, and a willingness to be vulnerable. Intentional school leaders at all levels model the trust they want their school community members to develop. Specifically, they demonstrate their trust in others and act consistently in order to be perceived as trustworthy. Trust building is integral to relationship building.

Bryk and Schneider (2002) researched trust in schools and found that schools with low student achievement always had low levels of trust. Conversely, most schools with high student achievement also demonstrated high levels of trust among their educational communities.

In *Coaching Conversations: Transforming Your School One Conversation at a Time* (Cheliotes & Reilly, 2010), we emphasized the importance of using coach-like skills to build trust and community. We stressed the importance of committed listening because this coach-like behavior conveys something important to the listener:

That they are valued, that you are open to their ideas even if you do not agree with them, and that you sincerely want to engage in a dialogue rather than a monologue. Through committed listening you are able to build relationships and trust. (p. 23)

Moreover, asking open-ended questions (those that cannot be answered with a *yes* or *no*) encourages those with whom you are speaking to engage in reflective thinking and creative solutions.

The following story is a powerful example of how just one coaching conversation built trust, a sense of community, and the development of personal responsibility within a previously difficult staff member.

## Better Late Than Never

### Linda Gross Cheliotes

When Bradley saw his assistant principal, Ellie, approach, he knew he was about to be chastised again for being late. After all, over a period of five years, he had collected forty-three reprimands in his personnel file for lateness. What he did not know was that Ellie intentionally had decided to have a coaching conversation with him instead.

During her own coaching sessions, Ellie expressed that she wanted to figure out a way to approach Bradley about his tardiness in a way that would have a real impact on changing his behavior. Clearly, another reprimand would make no difference to him. Instead, Ellie wanted to enter the conversation with positive intent. When she reflected upon what positives she could truthfully state about Bradley, she immediately remembered that he was an exceptionally talented teacher of English Language Learners (ELLs).

With this positive information, Ellie knew exactly how she would start the conversation. She scheduled an appointment with Bradley and told him that she would come to his classroom for the meeting. Ellie praised Bradley for the excellent progress his students were making and told him that they would profit even more from his teaching if he were on time every day. Ellie listened intently as he discussed a series of personal reasons for being late. The teacher became very emotional because no one had ever praised him for his work with students. He just received admonishments for his lateness. He then attempted to bargain with Ellie, promising he would get to school on time *four* days each week. She remained silent. The teacher then responded to his own proposal stating, "My students need me here on time *every* day of the week."

Next, Ellie asked him a powerful open-ended question, "What are your plans for being on time so your students profit from every minute of instruction?" Bradley reflected and said he could move some of his daily routines to the evening instead of the morning so he could keep his promise to be on time for work every day.

Because Ellie approached Bradley with positivity and trust rather than accusations, he developed his own plan for improvement and was on time every day for the remaining three months of the school year.

Even his colleagues found him more pleasant at work. Instead of always taking the opposite view of ideas they presented, Bradley began to accept his colleagues' plans and even added creative suggestions. Previously, the other teachers had resented Bradley because they had had to use their preparation time to cover his class when he was late. They now looked forward to working with him rather than avoiding confrontations. Bradley was helping to build school community and trust. Such was the power of a coach-leader's single coaching conversation!

## Coaching Insights

When faced with the dilemma of motivating Bradley to change his habit of tardiness, Ellie recognized that she would need to use a different approach with him than other administrators had in the past. She decided that it was very important to build a relationship of trust with Bradley and that this could best be accomplished by entering into a coaching conversation based on positive intent.

Ellie knew that Bradley was an excellent bilingual teacher and wondered if anyone had shared this information with him. She also realized that holding the conversation in his classroom rather than her office would likely feel more comfortable to the teacher. This tactic, too, was intentionally designed to foster trust and build a bond with Bradley. At the same time, as the school's leader, it was Ellie's responsibility to hold up the expectation that the teacher must be punctual each school day so that his students would have the full benefit of their teacher's skills in maximizing learning.

Once Ellie opened her conversation with a positive statement about Bradley while emphasizing the expectation that his students needed his full-time teaching expertise, his emotions were deeply touched by the assistant principal's comments. Creating a bond on an emotional level raised the trust level between the two. Bradley revealed some very personal reasons for his tardiness and his trust in Ellie led him to offer a solution—to arrive on time *four* days each week.

However, Ellie was committed to listening to Bradley and she wanted to avoid giving him direct orders or advice. Instead, she was silent while the teacher reflected on the conversation and the needs of his students. That is when he pledged to arrive at school every day on time for the benefit of his class. Because he had reached this conclusion on his own, he now had the motivation to carry out his promise.

In addition, Ellie recognized that since Bradley would be developing a new habit of punctuality, he would require a specific plan to follow. That is when she asked him the powerful open-ended question "What are your plans for being on time so your students profit from every minute of instruction?" Again, Ellie avoided advice and by staying silent, provided time for Bradley to reflect. He then was able to articulate very specific plans that would keep his spark of motivation activated.

Another extraordinary consequence of Ellie's coaching conversation with Bradley was that his interactions with his teaching colleagues improved, too. He was no longer the chronically late teacher whose class had to be covered by them until his arrival, and Bradley began to develop a spirit of trust and community with his fellow teachers. Instead of being defensive when working with them, he felt free to agree with them and to support their efforts.

As a consequence of Ellie's one powerful coaching conversation with Bradley, she not only motivated him to change a detrimental habit, but she also enhanced the trust level and sense of community throughout the school.

In our next story, you will notice that building trust and community in a school environment is a daily practice for coach-leaders who continually develop community and trust in their schools, setting the stage for meaningful reflective conversations and change. Moreover, by modeling positive intent and creating a culture of positivity, the coach-leader supports high goals for all students and high, positive expectations for all staff.

### Language Matters

#### Karen Anderson

Language matters! How you say things to others can lift them up or tear them down. Language that presumes the best in others builds trust and keeps commitment alive! As principal of a Montessori Academy in a large urban system, Lisa knows firsthand the challenges that can come from the bureaucracy and uncertainty of a large district. What she also knows for sure is that presuming positive intent can have a profound countereffect to feelings of isolation and being unappreciated that sometimes show up when working in a large system.

Not only does Lisa believe in the change-producing effect presuming positive intent can have, but she also practices it every day in her role as coach-leader. As is the case in most states, the spring of the year brings high-stakes testing and a frenzy that challenges the best in all of us. Knowing

*(Continued)*

(Continued)

this, Lisa is mindful of her language as she maintains the focus on both student performance and the confidence and efficacy of staff members as the test dates draw near.

One example of how Lisa walks the talk is exemplified in a communication she sent to her staff during this extremely stressful time. Consistently mirroring her belief in her staff, she addressed them as *Dear Exemplary Teacher*. Never taking her eye off the target to improve student performance, she raised the ante by shifting from proficiency on the state assessment to the higher standard of commended students as she had her exemplary teachers record the percentage of commended students for reading and math from Spring 2010 to a projection of commended students for spring of 2011. She used positive intent as the means for simultaneously holding up the expectations for high levels of performance.

Lisa personalizes each letter with the teacher's name and this message: "Thank you for all you do for students! I am *confident* that the spring 2011 commended results will reflect your smart work, dedication, and commitment to excellence!" The signature line reads *Your #1 Cheerleader* and closes with her handwritten signature. These expressions of positive intent are the coach-like behaviors that send the strong message "I believe in you! I trust you! I know you have a plan!"

While this is but one small example of how Lisa shows her staff how appreciative she is of their commitment and hard work, she consistently invites them to be their best self by believing in them, honoring their effort, and reinforcing their greatness. Lisa models what she wants most for the students in her school—a place that affirms and encourages the brilliance that resides within each of us.

## Coaching Insights

In this story, Lisa first reflected on her own mindset and clarified how she wanted to "be" or "show up" for others. She held a deep belief in the transformative power of positive rather than negative language. That is, she modeled positive intent. Lisa was also clear about the results she wanted for the school's students—that they would perform well enough on state assessments to receive a commended rating. Lisa kept this main idea in mind throughout her communications with staff members as she clearly articulated the standards and expectations of the work to be done. Finally, Lisa called on her teachers to be their best selves by inviting them to an even higher level of performance. She used positive intent to encourage staff to aim for a commended rating for their students rather than just proficient. In other words, she supported them in aiming for excellence rather than mediocrity. Through her positive efforts, Lisa created space for both trust and community as integral parts of her school's culture.

Our next story demonstrates that as a coach-leader, you may never realize the full positive impact you have on others. Utilizing committed listening, paraphrasing, positive intent, and reflective feedback within your school community provides the groundwork for building both trust and community. Just as a pebble thrown into water creates a ripple that reaches the far shores of the pond, your use of coach-leader skills ripples throughout your school community.

## The Safest Haven

### Dave Winans

Carol, the usually over-the-top positive client, began the coaching session with exasperation.

> I'm so fed up with insensitive parents! An eighth-grade girl came to school and was acting out even more than usual. I know the girl well; in fact, her mother had been a student of mine. We sat down with the girl and listened. Her father had been killed violently the night before but that wasn't what was upsetting her, since he had been sexually abusing the girl since she was nine. The girl didn't have a clue about what to do to help her little brother! Why was that poor girl sent to school with all of that weighing on her?

Before Carol got back to her usual coaching call rhythm, recounting positive incidents and events, she shared another example of a child who came to school after a traumatic family event. Soon, however, Carol

*(Continued)*

(Continued)

regained her typical coaching demeanor and shared celebrations since the previous coaching call. She identified incidents that had occurred in the past two weeks about which she now was laughing at herself. She shared excitement in applying an intervention for a group of teachers that had been effective for her. Carol marveled at the reduced distress in her life and attributed that to regular exercise alongside her best strategic partner, Mark (who also happens to be her husband). She clarified that she wasn't without stress, but the stress Carol now experienced was part of the desire to do specific things well, a very different experience than general anxiety and sleeplessness.

After thirty-five minutes, Carol blurted out, "Now I know why those kids were made to come to school! The parents weren't abandoning them; they were sending them to the safest place they know—they knew we would care for them!"

Carol and, through her, her school are trustworthy. The families of these two children respect Carol and the staff as, now, two generations have perceived competence, integrity, and personal regard. The children and their mothers know school to be a safe, nurturing place that insists upon results. And where there is trust, high achievement has a chance.

The coaching call stopped abruptly. Carol was late for a classroom visit—she was going to catch staff catch students doing good things!

## Coaching Insights

Until Carol had an opportunity for reflection during her coaching session, she had not realized the full impact of her coach-leader behaviors on the entire school community. She then realized that all of her efforts to build a trusting and trustworthy educational environment among her staff had also trickled down to the families whose children attended the school.

Her new insight was that parents and students trusted the school's staff to help them through both good and difficult times.

She was reenergized and recommitted to making her school a safe haven for the entire school community.

In the next story, you will learn how one school leader used her coach-like skills to create a supportive working relationship between home and school, with a child profiting from the newly developed positive relationship.

A major challenge for many school leaders is establishing trust between school staff and parents. This is especially true when working with students who have special learning needs. Each side has knowledge and skills that the other side may not. Instead of combining their expertise and efforts to help individual children succeed in school, the relationships between home and school may become toxic and adversarial.

## From Parent Intrusion to Parent Involvement

### Diana Williams

Principal Amy presented to her coach the dilemma of being caught in the middle of tensions between a teacher and a parent of a student with Tourette's syndrome. The parent complained about the lack of communication and responsiveness on the part of the teacher and the school. The teacher complained that the parent was overbearing and intrusive. The principal often found herself as the buffer between the parent and the teacher, who was sometimes intimidated by the mother. The parent had threatened lawsuits over procedural questions and extra services for her son. She frequently checked in with the principal's supervisors to request services and information. The principal felt betrayed and blindsided by these perceived complaints, as she had always maintained an open door policy for parents and their concerns. Also, the principal and school had worked hard to develop antibullying strategies, as this child was a target of frequent bullying behavior.

With her coach, the principal explored multiple options for strategies to work with this situation that was causing considerable tension between

*(Continued)*

(Continued)

the teacher and the parent and considerable stress for the principal in trying to mediate this situation. In determining what she wanted, the principal determined that she wanted the parent and teacher to work in partnership to best meet the needs of this student. The principal wanted to establish trust and rapport with the parent and also offer support to the very excellent teacher who had worked hard to develop innovative strategies for working with this child. The ultimate goal was to get the parent and the teacher talking with and cooperating with each other.

On the plus side, the mother had come out of the workplace in order to stay at home with her children and manage her special needs fourth grader with Tourette's syndrome. The mother had become quite knowledgeable about Tourette's and wanted to be a partner with the school staff in the education of her child.

By engaging the parent in a trusting and supportive environment rather than an adversarial one, the parent eventually felt safe in sharing the struggles she was having at home with her child and came to look upon the principal and the school as a resource.

One of the strategies that developed was to invite the mother to volunteer at the school and attend special education meetings and bring back information to the school. The parent wrote a piece for the newsletter about Tourette's. This parent became a primary supporter of the school as she looked forward to being involved in a meaningful way.

The principal had to work with the teacher to encourage her to work with the parent. The teacher made more time for parent meetings to discuss the child with Tourette's syndrome and began to understand the mother's perspective and the difficulty of raising a child with Tourette's. As the relationship between the teacher and parent grew, the teacher was more willing to collaborate and elicit ideas from her grade-level team. The team shared strategies for managing transitional time with this student. The teacher engaged in professional development to become more knowledgeable about Tourette's, and the teacher felt less isolated in dealing with a difficult student. As a result of their shared knowledge and increased trust, everyone worked together on clear goals in the student's Individualized Education Program (IEP).

## Coaching Insights

Before the principal could resolve the issue of an intrusive parent working against a defensive teacher, she needed to clarify what she herself wanted, how she wanted the relationship between home and school to be. Amy, the principal, already recognized that a cooperative environment enhances student success while adversarial relationships detract from a student's success.

Amy realized that there were significant communication barriers between the parent of the child with Tourette's syndrome and school personnel. She understood that a series of meaningful coaching conversations would help establish the trust required. Amy comprehended that sometimes complaints mask great passion around an issue. It was important to listen committedly to the parent's and teacher's words and emotions so that their negative energy could be channeled and focused on finding mutually acceptable solutions.

Once both sides began to really listen to each other, their trust and cooperation grew, recognizing that they both wanted what was best for the child involved.

### Key Ideas for Building Trust and Community

- Clarify what you value and how you want "to be" (your emotions, demeanor, your mindset) in your interactions with others.
- Be deliberate about having positive intent and presuppositions in mind for your coaching conversations.
- Look for and acknowledge the strengths in people. You then relate differently, more respectfully, with them. You have greater potential for influence and understanding when there is respect in the relationship.
- Listen fully and with commitment as people speak.
- Provide space for silence in conversations. The other person will then have an opportunity to reflect on the situation being discussed.
- Avoid advice. Instead, ask powerful, open-ended questions that require more than a *yes* or *no* answer. By doing so you will provide space for reflection and creative thinking by others.
- Be clear about articulating and holding up high expectations. This builds trust and a sense of community.
- Encourage others to develop their own solutions and action plans that fit within stated expectations, goals, and values.

## Your Learning

1. What in these stories resonates with you? Why?

2. What challenges around trust and community building are you facing?

3. What steps could you take that would increase trust and rapport within your school community?

_____

_____

_____

_____

_____

_____

_____

_____

_____

_____

_____

_____

_____

_____

_____

_____

_____

# Holding Up High Expectations for All

*High achievement always takes place in the framework of high expectation.*

—Charles F. Kettering

*Efforts and courage are not enough without purpose and direction.*

—John F. Kennedy

Commitment to high expectations emerges as leaders build trust and develop a sense of community within their schools. High trust and strong community create an environment where individuals within the school begin to hold themselves accountable for reaching the expectations and standards they hold in common. High expectations attract more energy and commitment when they connect to values we jointly believe rather than to obligations we must fulfill.

> High expectations attract more energy and commitment when they connect to values we jointly believe rather than to obligations we must fulfill.

So showing how the expectations connect with core values and personal visions help "enroll" staff in commitment. Then it is important for the leader to work with *all* staff members as *partners,* with strengths to contribute rather than *problems* to be fixed.

When principals are assigned to new schools or teacher leaders take on new roles or responsibilities within a group of colleagues, they are often responsible for holding up and *modeling* high standards and best practices. This can be difficult to do. It means previous relationships change. It means building trust and rapport in a new and different way. It means establishing leadership within a peer group in a way that focuses on being a trusted *influencer*, not a *boss*.

In the first story, "Pat" is assigned as new principal in a school with average to good student success. Yet she sees areas in which she wants to challenge the veteran staff to even higher standards. Read how she navigates the tricky balance of building trust and relationships while challenging the status quo.

## Finding Your Leadership Voice

### Marceta Fleming Reilly

Pat was a new principal at a school with a veteran staff. She was concerned about resistance among the staff to the new ideas she wanted to bring to the school and frustrated with their "games." Instead, she wanted her staff members to be true collaborators and for them to have a strong commitment to good instruction.

When she thought about what she wanted the adults to be doing in her school, she honed it into three clear statements:

1. I want staff to support and collaborate with each other.
2. I want student learning to be the focus of instruction.
3. I want staff to create common learning goals, assessments, and performance criteria within and across grade levels.

When she communicated this vision to her leadership team, she became very excited. Members of the leadership team embraced many of the concepts Pat described in her vision, and they spontaneously generated ideas to support it.

By sharing her vision with the leadership team, Pat found that many of her key teachers wholeheartedly agreed with her ideas. This gave her confidence and courage to move forward, sharing the vision with the rest of the staff.

Over the next few months, Pat's conversations began to "enroll" and ignite the energy of her staff with the exception of the fifth-grade team. She continued to feel resistance from them. Whenever she was planning to work with them, her thinking would start with predicting how badly they would respond. Then it would move to figuring out ways to confront them and be authoritative in her position.

She wanted to reframe her work with the fifth-grade teachers. So she began to think about the strengths that the fifth-grade teachers had which would fit into her vision for the school. She was able to list strengths for each teacher. But it was difficult for her to approach them based upon their strengths rather than working from the conflicts. She was so used to seeing them as adversaries that it was hard to see them as allies.

She thought about ways she had worked with children and other groups of teachers to support and build on strengths rather than working from deficits. This broke through her resistance and gradually she became very clear about what she wanted from this team:

- Talk about student work and exchange sound teaching ideas.
- Teach units together.
- Share strengths by talking about instructional philosophies.
- Learn from each other.

These became the expectations for all the grade-level teams. Pat included these expectations in some team-building/trust-building activities at faculty meetings, and she continued to set clear expectations about what a new, collaborative culture could look like for her school. Slowly her fifth-grade team began to be more cooperative and engaged.

Pat's desire was to balance setting clear expectations without being a dictator. Her work with her building leadership team had paid off. There was high morale and positive interaction with her and among the members. They were responding well to her leadership—recognizing her strengths in

(Continued)

(Continued)

curriculum and instruction—and moving forward without complaint. She found that setting clear expectations and being explicit with her vision was very helpful to the staff. Even the difficult teachers became less argumentative and more receptive to the changes she wanted.

## Coaching Insights

At the beginning, Pat was very frustrated because a few staff members were continuously arguing about her decisions and pushing back about the boundaries. She learned that it was important to be clear about what she wanted (her vision) and to acknowledge the values and strengths she had to draw upon. Pat spent time answering these questions about her vision:

- What does my vision look like?
- What does it sound like?
- With whom is it most important to share my vision?

These questions helped her think about ways to share her clear vision with others.

Then Pat considered the strengths of each of the fifth-grade teachers. This was a new perspective for her and gave her a new vantage point. It was difficult for her, but once she shifted to thinking of them as allies for teaching children, her attitude and her edge softened. She was able to approach the group differently—more respectfully—and they responded to her differently. She got different results than she had in the past.

Through this work, Pat began to focus on leading with her strengths. She became less concerned about beating back adversaries and more focused on creating a school team.

Pat grew from being a person who was frustrated because a few staff members were continuously arguing about her decisions and not accepting her leadership to a person who clearly articulated her expectations and values while listening with care to the needs of others. She sought the win-win solutions wherever she could as long as her basic beliefs were not compromised. Pat found her leadership voice and challenged staff to higher expectations for all students.

In the next story a principal holds up clear expectations and supports staff in reaching them by asking reflective questions.

## Being Contagious Makes You Better

### Karen Anderson

What principal would not want high-quality instruction in every classroom of the school EVERY day of the year? That means even when holidays are coming, testing is nearing, there are only fifteen days between one break and another, or the end of the year is in sight. Every minute is precious learning time!

That is exactly what Angie believed as she noticed that the quality of lesson planning was dipping to an all-time low as the second semester of school was beginning. She resolved to do something about it!

When her coach asked what criteria had been articulated as expectations for high-quality lesson planning, there was an extended pause. Angie immediately recognized the issue. Her articulated expectations had been about the logistics of lesson planning—do them, address all curricular areas, complete them online every week by Monday at 8:00 a.m.

What she wanted was to return to the standards and expectations for her desired outcome—evidence of regular and consistent high-quality lesson planning. Quickly, she developed four measures for her goal that she would address in her faculty meeting scheduled for that very afternoon:

1. Meets student needs

2. Aligns with the district scope and sequence

3. Offers sufficient detail for others to successfully teach it (including me)

4. Matches what I see when I come into your classroom

It was in response to the question "How will you monitor implementation of this best practice strategy?" that Angie got to the crux of her plan. She wanted to ensure there was a balance of tension and support in her follow-up behaviors to get what she wanted. Previously, she had offered no feedback to teachers' lesson plans. Reflective feedback was what Angie identified as the means to her end. She had previously learned there were three options for reflective feedback—ask clarifying questions, offer value potential statements, or ask reflective questions for possibility. She knew the attributes of the questions were that they were open-ended rather than *yes/no*, they presumed positive intent, and they promoted the thinking of the other person.

*(Continued)*

(Continued)

She committed to the accomplishment of a new goal—"owning the skill" of reflective feedback—because she believed it would provoke her teachers' thinking around quality lesson planning. She also believed it held the greatest potential for stretching her teachers who already went above and beyond the standard.

Toward this end, she collected samples of the exact reflective feedback language she used with teachers on the current week's lesson plans and brought it to the coaching conversation for discussion and improvement. Her reflection was that value potential statements were easy for her and that the reflective questions for possibility were where she wanted to focus her attention. She also noted that she was creating a response pattern of extending a value potential statement as a lead-in to a reflective question. She gave the following examples:

- For a strong teacher who goes above and beyond, she asked, "The format of your lesson plans (Today the students will . . . ) shows that you are thinking deeply about the lessons you will be teaching. Knowing you are trying something new, what are the anticipated results of this new format?"
- Another time, she wanted to "hold up the expectation" to give a little nudge. So she asked, "Knowing your students so well, what differentiation strategies are you thinking you want to try?" She wanted this to support the teacher in considering important measures for a high-quality lesson.
- For the teacher who submitted incomplete lesson plans, she offered this feedback: "As you compare your lesson plans to the articulated standards and expectations for high quality, what are you thinking will be your next steps to meet these expectations?" This would help the teacher focus her thinking about next steps.

Angie was energized. "I can't wait to practice my reflective feedback today!" Imagine the growth of Angie's staff AND the contagiousness of her own enthusiasm by leading in such a proactive way!

## Coaching Insights

Angie moved from seeing a problem to creating a vision of what she wanted: effective instruction EVERY day. She honed that even more specifically by focusing on lesson planning as a key element of effective instruction every day. She got very clear about the criteria she had for a high-quality lesson plan. Then she held up these standards and expectations in daily conversations with teachers. Teachers knew what she wanted and Angie worked hard to sustain this focus.

Angie created tension and support about the changes she wanted to see. The tension was the time and energy she spent talking with the staff about lesson planning. The support came as she used language that was affirming and presumed the best of others. She planned her comments with care as she observed teachers, and her questions were open-ended and thought provoking.

Now let's look at a principal who was assigned to a failing school and created a committed team of dedicated professionals.

## Turning Around a Failing School

### Sandee Crowther

Laura was reassigned to a school in the district that was being restructured since the school had failed to make Adequate Yearly Progress (AYP) for multiple years. She felt the key to success would be teamwork and changing the culture in the school. She sensed the newly constituted staff had the ability within themselves to make a collective difference for these students. Rather than dictating what would be done, she used focused questions and modeled high expectations that the staff would create a successful school.

Through ongoing discussions with staff, she raised various questions:

- How do we demonstrate belief in each other as well as our students?
- How do we show support for each other?
- How do we know if students are improving?
- How do we know how we are doing as a staff or as a team of teachers at a grade level?
- How do we get parents more involved?

Staff members brainstormed together and created a code of conduct for the building that they all agreed to support. She then asked them how they would help the students understand this code of conduct.

*(Continued)*

(Continued)

Teachers gave their ideas and came up with not only initial plans but also ongoing ways to reinforce the ideas.

Teachers agreed that the various types of achievement data before them were not what they would want or expect and agreed to monitor data on a regular basis and make adjustments within their teams. They became a school that collectively worked on developing a positive learning community with high expectations for all. Laura's classroom observations and supportive notes which also often included some clarifying questions, helped to build the support and accountability for the community of learners. For example, she would ask, "How do you know that your students understood the expected outcome for today's lesson?"

After making AYP in the first spring, the leadership team knew the importance of celebrating success with students, with staff members, and with parents. Laura continued by asking important questions:

- What helped us to be successful?
- How do we want to continue to improve?
- What plans will we put in place for next year?

The data from the school's Climate and Culture surveys done two times each year continue to demonstrate that the staff and students see vast improvements in the culture of the school and take ownership for what has been created. They feel the leadership changed the climate to "uplifting and cheerful." Staff members express that they are very involved in decision-making and that they are trusted to make sound, professional decisions. Staff members were very positive about being recognized and valued.

For the second year in a row, the school made AYP and is now no longer labeled "on improvement." The principal with her coach-like skills was able to get ownership and commitment from staff and supported them in the process. Their new goal is to go from "good to great!"

## Coaching Insights

Laura started with the belief that individuals can create what will work for them, once they are clear about the *collective* standards and expectations. She did not dictate what would be done, but instead, she spent time collaborating with the staff, developing their *collective* vision for the school. She asked open-ended, thought-filled questions that moved the staff to articulate their core beliefs about students and staff.

Laura was strong on accountability, but she used it as an "interesting conversation" rather than a hammer. She had frequent conversations with faculty about her observations of instruction and then asked the *teachers* to analyze and take meaning from the data that emerged. Her approach was to ask them what *they* saw in the data, not to tell them what *she* saw in it. She was drawing out their professional expertise and showing that she depended upon it.

Laura was quick to celebrate successes and show appreciation for the hard work of students, staff, parents, and community. Yet, she also understood that celebration is an ideal catalyst to think about what factors created the conditions for the success and plan what steps will continue the good results.

Laura led from behind and drew out the best in her faculty. She treated them as professionals and tapped into their buried dreams about what being a teacher means. She rekindled their desire to make a difference for students.

### Key Ideas for Holding Up High Expectations for Staff

- Share standards and expectations as a "vision."
- Connect the values held by others to elements of your vision. This spreads excitement and ignites the staff.
- Look for the strengths in people rather than focusing on their deficits. It provides greater potential for influence and understanding, and brings more energy and commitment to the solution.
- Talk about the standards and expectations frequently.
  - Ask how they are measuring success.
  - Ask about their celebrations and debrief about the elements that made it so.
  - Ask about their challenges and probe for specific barriers contributing to them.
  - Ask what they are learning from implementation.
  - Ask what indicators of change will have the most impact for them.
- Encourage staff to collaborate to share ideas and increase their options.
- Use the words of others (gleaned from these conversations) to describe and motivate the group.
- Notice even small successes and celebrate!

## Your Learning

1. What in these stories resonates with you? Why?

2. What are the standards and expectations you want to hold up with your school community?

3. How might you communicate these standards and expectations without giving advice or directives?

# Changing
# How We Change

*We must become the change we wish to see in the world.*

—Mahatma Gandhi

*There's a difference between interest and commitment. When you're interested in doing something, you do it only when it's convenient. When you're committed to something, you accept no excuses; only results.*

—Kenneth Blanchard

Your world is constantly in a state of flux. More often than not you need the support, cooperation, and collaboration of others to implement changes that will help students in your school community achieve at high levels. Surely your goals for improvement are worthy, research supports your strategies, and much training has taken place. Yet, why is it so hard to keep on track or to get others on board? Our first story will provide you with some clues.

### I Want to . . . But

### Linda Gross Cheliotes

Antonio was full of creative ideas for his suburban school and for himself, professionally and personally. As the lead assistant principal, he wanted to become the principal of his school when the current leader was transferred. He knew he could effect many changes that would lead his school to higher levels of excellence. Yet, when the opportunity arose to move up, Antonio was missing one essential credential required and was passed over for the principalship.

On the personal side, Antonio had dreams of earning a doctorate in education at a prestigious Ivy League university. He knew he was intelligent enough and experienced enough to be accepted into the program. Somehow, time kept passing and he never quite got around to filling out the application. Instead, he occupied his time working on the moment-to-moment crises that developed each day in his school.

Why would such a bright, resourceful young man fail to take even the simple steps necessary to achieve his dreams? Through individual coaching, Antonio began to realize that he was afraid to change, that he even resisted change. Logically, he recognized that the work related to the changes he sought would take very little time—filling out some paperwork, writing an essay, perhaps networking with people who could help him advance his career and education. And still he procrastinated and focused his time and energy on day-to-day activities.

How often have you acted like Antonio? You are quite capable of determining the path to your goals, yet you become sidetracked by daily routines and avoid following actions that will lead you forward. How often have you worked with teachers who have attended a number of trainings, yet they fail to implement new strategies that they say they understand? What causes this resistance to change?

## Coaching Insights

Let's examine why we avoid change. Karen Dyer and Jacqueline Carothers, authors of *The Intuitive Principal* (2000), provide us with important clues:

Effective leaders are astute at reading the environment. They recognize that despite the ever present opportunity to initiate change through the exertion of positional power, constituents will commit to making only those changes viewed as relevant, feasible, and worthy of trust. (p. 42)

Educators at all levels recognize that through the power of one's position, others may be ordered to change. However, unless individuals actually commit to the new expectations, they are unlikely to fully support changes, and there is little hope of new goals, strategies, plans, or ways of being becoming part of the culture of the

> The hardest part of educational change is not how to start it, but how to make it last and spread.
>
> —Hargreaves & Shirley, 2009

school or district. Andy Hargreaves and Dennis Shirley (2009) succinctly state the problem, "The hardest part of educational change is not how to start it, but how to make it last and spread" (p. 94).

David Rock (2006) describes how our behaviors are hard-wired habits in our brains. Even when we logically understand the need to change, our brain readily returns us to those familiar hard-wired neural pathways. Rock describes how it is very difficult or even impossible to erase these habituated neural pathways. However, change is possible when we create new neural pathways and practice new habits. Rock states, "Our brain tries to make whatever we are sensing or thinking fit into our existing mental models" (p. 16). He goes on to say, "New habits take time, but not that much . . . Positive feedback is essential" (p. 24). In other words, we can support and encourage changes in people's thinking "by helping them clearly identify the insights they would like to hardwire, and over time reminding them about these insights" (p. 25).

In the case of Antonio, he cognitively recognized the need for change, yet he lacked trust in himself. It was easier for him to think about *If only* . . . scenarios in his head than to risk failure. He would set attainable goals, yet follow the familiar hard-wired habits he had practiced for many years.

What are your thoughts so far about the change process? Perhaps you are saying to yourself, "This all sounds fine, but the authors don't know how difficult it is to get people in *our* school to accept new ways of doing things. Many staff members here resist even simple changes." Or, "There are power struggles between the school's administrators and teachers. Supervisors expect changes in teaching strategies and curriculum that we already know won't work." Or possibly, "We think we are already doing a great job with our students and changes are unnecessary." You might even be thinking, "I would like to change some of my work habits, but every time I try, I fail to follow through on the promises I make to myself."

Read the story of Jenny to discover how she overcame resistance to change in herself and in her colleagues.

## The Crucial "Aha" Moment

### Gina Marx

She was bright and everything she did was 100 mph. Jenny was an assistant principal in a large urban high school who was charged with teaching two math courses to students in addition to her leadership duties. She shared in our coaching calls how she thought she overwhelmed her colleagues, and her principal had even told her that she came off to her coworkers as too blunt and intimidating. Jenny said she didn't care, though. Yet, the topics she would want to discuss seemed to always be around how various colleagues were "driving her nuts." She shared emotions such as frustration and anger at not getting credit when she had helped a colleague and the coworker "took all the credit"; yet she said she didn't need to be recognized. We had discussed the value of choosing her words with positive intent, to help build the efficacy of those around her, but she had strong feelings around the need to do things quickly, and it was more efficient and faster to "just tell people what they need to do." She tried out the language between our sessions, but felt one colleague was so "stupid" she didn't feel like she could truly believe in that person's abilities. As her coach, I pointed out to Jenny that she had shared with me how she loved her high school students and how funny they were and how smart they were.

"You love teaching and you are good at it," I said.

"Thank you," she replied. "I do think I'm a very good teacher."

"I'll bet that some students drive you nuts, or they are not as bright as other students, but you still have patience with them and never give

up on helping them to do better and better and learn at high levels."
Jenny went on to talk animatedly about how this statement was true and
how much she enjoyed working with all types of students.

"So," I said very slowly. "As a leader in your building, whose job it is
to lead others and take them to higher levels of effectiveness, how is
teaching students different from working with and teaching your adult
colleagues?" I asked.

Silence.

More silence.

For the first time in all of our conversations, Jenny spoke slowly.
"Ohhh . . . I see what you are getting at. I'm going to need to think about
this."

This was a huge "aha" moment for Jenny. We followed up with
conversation around the type of leader she wanted to be. I suggested to her
that her brain functioned at a very high level, and that she may never work
with other adults as smart as she was. But understanding her core values,
and embracing mental models around leadership and the use of coaching
language, she could become a coach-leader. Jenny was now on her way.

## Coaching Insights

Jenny's thinking and behavior at the beginning of this story are
very typical for most of us. How often do you make assumptions
about others that if you can see the necessity and value of a plan,
model, or goal, others should be able to understand, too! On the
other hand, you grasp that students have different learning styles,
interests, and skills, and you are motivated to adjust teaching strategies and materials to meet the unique needs of each student.

So it is with adults, too. Our thinking and behaviors are hard-
wired and we need to accept, learn, and practice new ways of thinking and behaving. Such was Jenny's big "aha" moment. With her
coach's support, she began to recognize that most of her colleagues
did not operate the same way she did. As a result, it was hard for
Jenny to get buy-in from them for her ideas, vision, and plans. Jenny
began to realize that her colleagues were similar to her students—
they were unique individuals, and Jenny would need to hold coaching conversations with them to encourage their thinking and support
them as they practiced developing new neural pathways, new habits.

You might imagine Jenny using her new insights to hold conversations with coworkers in which she would listen deeply to their concerns, fear of new risks, and attitudes about proposed changes. She would paraphrase their thinking so she and they would be on the same page, and she would ask powerful, open-ended questions that would lead to reflective thinking, resulting in the exploration of possibilities for implementing changes. In other words, she would discuss options and plans until her colleagues discovered personal reasons to buy into proposed changes.

Once coworkers began practicing new habits of mind, Jenny could provide them with reflective feedback that helped them clarify their thinking, express the value or value potential of their new behaviors, and ask them reflective questions to reinforce or adjust their new neural pathways.

In our next story, you will learn how providing others with unexpected positive feedback may open the door to change.

## Changing a Relationship Through Language

### Kathy Kee

Lakeisha was thrilled to become the new principal of an elementary school. She had been preparing for many years for the role. She had been a lead teacher, a reading coach, and an assistant principal.

Lakeisha believes in the power of coaching and is aware of the impact of language on others. In this new role, she strives every day to be a coach-leader. In her conversations with her coach, she regularly wants to think through and rehearse her words, knowing the potential in each conversation.

Recently, her district adopted policies that added criteria for continuing staff contracts, which included student performance levels and effective classroom instruction. A criterion that flags personnel for nonrenewal or even blocks transfers includes the addition of any negative documentation.

Lakeisha's conversation with her coach began with these surprising words, "I'm so fed up! I've got three teachers who are habitually late. I have talked with them about the impact on their students and other staff but the behavior continues. It's like they just don't get it, such selfish behavior, not to mention they are not meeting the expectations of their contract! I'm sick of it. I'm just going to write them up!"

Her coach acknowledged the principal's frustration and disappointment. She affirmed Lakeisha's high standards for professional behavior that she holds herself to as well as her staff. When asked how critical these teachers were to student success in her school, Lakeisha reflected on the three teachers and candidly said two were weak or borderline, but one teacher, a fifth-grade teacher, was outstanding. She continued to identify the teacher's gifts in reading and math. Her students are very motivated and have potential for great success. In no time, Lakeisha realized that the fifth-grade teacher was worth an investment in her. The teacher was excellent and losing her would be unfavorable.

When asked what opportunities she had taken to tell this teacher how valuable she was to the school and the gifts Lakeisha saw in her, in a moment of insight, Lakeisha realized she really had not shared with her any personal comments or affirmations.

Lakeisha knew the next question would be, "How are you thinking you would like to have a conversation with her to affirm her value and ask for her compliance with time expectations?"

For the next several minutes Lakeisha and her coach tossed out many options for approaching the teacher. Soon Lakeisha chose what she believed was her best approach. As agreed, her timeline was to speak to the teacher before the end of the week—only three days away.

On the next call, Lakeisha was excited about what she was witnessing. She could hardly wait to share the details of their conversation. She began by asking the teacher if she had a few minutes to talk about an important issue, and when the teacher agreed, Lakeisha told her what exceptional qualities she was seeing in her planning and teaching that was producing successful students. Lakeisha intentionally was very specific and continued by saying how she had grown to see her as an instructional role model to other staff members. As she continued, she said, "Mrs. Gomez, I am faced with some serious budget decisions this year and some members of this staff will probably be released or transferred. As principals have begun to prepare, there are many questions being asked about teachers around the district. Who is good, who is not, etc. I have been happy to share with those who have inquired

*(Continued)*

(Continued)

about you, your effective teaching and responsiveness to students. The *only thing*," Lakeisha said with animated hesitation, "I feel I must also be honest and share your tendency to be late. I just hate it. So given the potential for these budget implications, I need your help. I'm feeling a little like Jerry McGuire here but... help me... help you... I want only to have outstanding things to say about your qualities."

Mrs. Gomez immediately began to apologize and promised she would get her act together and stop being tardy. Lakeisha simply offered her belief in her teacher and thanked her for her time.

In the on-going weeks and months, every call began with, "She is still on time!" or "I am drop-dead amazed!" Lakeisha and her coach laughed and cheered together at the amazement of the change. Lakeisha said that if change in people was this profound all the time, we could change the world with coaching. She shares that each day when she sees that the teacher is in her class with time to spare, she frequently mumbles to herself—five weeks of miracles; seven weeks of miracles; fourteen weeks of miracles. As of June 1st, the teacher had been on time every day since their conversation on January 4th!

## Coaching Insights

Change is more than having a vision, sharing it with others, and then keeping tabs on who is or is not following the specified change process. A coach-leader reflects about team members and holds coaching conversations with them that reflect their individuality. What gifts does each person bring to the situation? How could each person be approached in a manner that reinforces their beliefs that they matter?

Neuroscience today tells us that people do change dramatically when they see the benefit to themselves and connected to a bigger purpose. They change when they feel believed in, when they feel valued, when they have a choice—the choice to be their best self.

The final story in this chapter reinforces the concept of positive intent as an important coach-leader tool in encouraging others to change.

## Acting Out My Future—Life Is Just a Performance

### Joan Hearne

After twenty-five years in her profession, Vickie, an assistant principal in a middle school, shared with her coach, "When I was a child, I wanted to be an actress, but I found my stage with children when I started teaching. Recently, I learned to use positive intent, *intentionally*. This transformed my life even outside of school. I stopped being personal and using emotion-filled words, blaming, or shaming. Even when I am not in the moment, positive intent pulls me into it."

Using this new-found tool, Vickie shared that she began to use positive intent with her students. Setting those expectations high for all children was a common daily routine for her, but once in awhile, some students just defied their potential.

Jason was one of those students, engaged in his own agenda; he was frequently absent, seldom on time with assignments, and on the verge of retention. Vickie had developed a very good relationship with Jason over the last several years, but her good intentions had not changed his academic interests or his behaviors in any way.

One day she took him aside and shared a dream she had, that of him being an influence in school and looking like a professional student. Knowing of an upcoming visit by the newly elected school chancellor, who was from that very neighborhood and went to this school, she asked if he would be her escort the next day during the visit. Based on his past behaviors, Vickie decided that his being her escort would allow her to be on top of his every move, while allowing him some positive attention. After a call to his home discussing the plans with his parents, she was anxious to see if he would even participate.

Jason, wearing a new pair of slacks and dress shirt, arrived early the next day. He made a point to visit several teachers prior to finding Vickie, and of course, they complimented him on his attire. This affirmation and attention resulted in a seventh-grade boy arriving at school in dress clothes and upgraded, appropriate behavior. He was ready for his job of escorting the assistant principal around when the chancellor, along with an entourage, arrived. This student, whose usual behaviors were not compliant, successful, or attending, managed to become a professional student for a day.

*(Continued)*

(Continued)

Not only was his behavior very appropriate, but he also found himself in the middle of the attention and the photos; he was even featured on the TV news that evening. This experience allowed a space for new behaviors to emerge, although, it is too soon to tell. Vickie continues to expect good things to happen through her advocacy and focuses using positive intent to affirm Jason's appropriate behaviors. It pays to share our dreams with students. They may just try *acting them out!*

## Coaching Insights

Before learning to use the skill of positive intent in her conversations, Vickie would often belittle, blame, or shame others into some form of compliant behavior. Of course, the outcomes would not last at all. This "sage on the stage" moved from acts to focusing on words and sentences, allowing the tool of positive intent to provide a suitable stage for each conversation with either a staff member or a student. Often our students and staff members *do* live up to our expectations, but what are we expecting? If we expect them to fail or behave poorly, they are likely to do just that. However, if we assume positive intentions about others, they are likely to act out these positive expectations, too. With positive intent we may see many changes.

---

### Key Points for Changing How We Change

- Listen with commitment when others are resistant to change.
- Recognize that it takes time to create new neural pathways and habits of mind.
- Presume positive intent that each person has the ability and willingness to change, develop solutions, and plan.
- Ask others open-ended questions that cause deep reflection about the proposed changes and open up possibilities for solutions.
- Provide support and encouragement for change by others through reflective feedback.
- Create a trusting environment in which all constituents feel safe taking risks.

## Your Learning

1. Which parts of these stories resonate with you? Why?

2. What changes would you like to see in yourself or in your school community?

3. What coach-like strategies will you use to motivate yourself and others to change?

# Getting Genuine Buy-In

*Framing Expectations*
*to Support Change*

*The best way to inspire people to superior performance is to convince them by everything you do and by your everyday attitude that you are wholeheartedly supporting them.*

—Harold S. Geneen

*There is only one way . . . to get anybody to do anything. And that is by making the other person want to do it.*

—Dale Carnegie

For most of my (Marceta) career, I have been in the role of "change agent" within the school districts where I have worked. In my early days, I was a teacher activist, organizing bargaining units in my district and sometimes stridently challenging board members or administrators. When I won a seat on the local school board, I fought to bring new instructional practices to the classrooms and had little tolerance for teachers and administrators who did not keep up with the latest theories and practices in education.

As principal of a school, I had the power to *make* staff members comply with my requests. But I knew that I wanted more than *compliance*; I wanted enthusiasm, energy, and effort—in other words—I wanted *commitment!*

So it was in my role as superintendent that I learned my most important lessons about how to *really* make changes that stick. I learned that it is first about showing respect and building trust. Only then would others be willing to listen to and follow me. It was the difference between getting compliance and creating commitment.

Our first story in this chapter is about a high school principal who gained solid commitment from his staff by showing them in everything he did that he supported them.

## Reflected Glory

### Sue Kidd

"A cheerleader," that is what he calls himself, "a cheerleader." This tall, rugged, quiet, rancher on the weekends and high school principal during the rest of his life describes himself as just that, a cheerleader. And even more interesting is that is exactly how his 200 students and 25 high school staff also describe him. Not the stand up and chant kind of fellow, not the rah-rah-rah leader but the holder of *high expectations* for everyone and the leader who creates a deep sense of trust that he will be there—he's got your back.

When we first started working together, he says that he was very good at telling people what to do—and how to do it. I wonder...Over time, he has found it more effective to listen, just listen. As you enter his building, you find him standing in the front hall, quietly listening to students, to teachers, asking questions and then listening.

What is he listening for? As the school implemented a new curriculum and all teachers were expected to integrate new teaching practices into their lessons, he was listening for a change in the culture and the climate of the school. He believed in Guskey's (2000) paradigm, "If we first change classroom practices, then student learning will change, which leads to a change in teacher's attitudes and beliefs" (p. 139).

He was listening for those subtle changes in the ways that students relate to one another and listening to the conversations that teachers were having with students and among themselves. His questions were clarifying and reflective, "How did you teach that concept and what did you see the students doing?"

When staff members come to him with concerns about the "new way of doing things," he listens for the clues that then guide his action. Do they need more support from another teacher to really see how to teach in this way? What pieces are they missing? When staff members agree that a change is needed and that they will make that change, his assumption is that they just need a bit more information or support to move ahead.

And who is the first person to open the doors of the school to visitors, to share his learning with other administrators, and to invite students to talk about their experiences? The "cheerleader" knows that public presentation deepens reflection and commitment. It opens the conversation, may require a bit of cleaning up along the way, but it also provides an opportunity for celebration—a celebration led by a tall, rugged cheerleader.

## Coaching Insights

This principal is exhibiting "quiet leadership." He creates buy-in by showing total trust and respect for the teachers, parents, and students in his school. His staff wants to follow him because they do not want to disappoint him or make him doubt his faith in them to reach the expectations he has for them.

He is clear about the expectations and the differences he believes the changes will make for the students. He listens deeply for clues that could help his people implement the new initiative better. Then he collaborates with them to provide the additional information, training, and support they desire.

This principal understands that he does not need to be the expert in *how* to implement the change with students. He just needs to be very clear about the student outcomes he wants and keep the conversation going about the bigger picture. What results are teachers getting? What refinements do they think would get them closer to the target? By trusting and supporting his staff, he is sharing power and earning great dividends in the "trust bank" of the community.

The next story is about a principal who is challenged by a music teacher who does not buy into a new district policy.

## Scoring With the Music Teacher

### Kathy Kee

Gary was very upset and frustrated. His day began with his music teacher bounding into his office with her already prepared list of music for the upcoming holiday program. As he glanced at the list, he immediately recognized that her selections did not align with the most current policy requiring that holiday music mirror the many rich cultures of the school.

Reacting to her "this is how we have always done it" language and attitude, he informed the long-time music teacher that the lineup was unacceptable and did not meet the requirements of policy. Instantly, her anger was loudly emotional as she scolded him with comments about her long history of using the music, her knowledge of policy, her choice of selections used for years, and the added caustic remark that the program had already been approved by her program director. How dare he challenge her!

Gary informed her, trying hard to maintain his self-control, that her selections did not meet the requirements of policy and she would have to start over. With that, the music teacher stormed from his office yelling she would take this matter over his head.

Gary was so frustrated with this teacher who he felt was used to doing whatever she wanted, viewing herself as the authority, and quite frankly, accustomed to running roughshod over most everyone. Now he was going to have to have another meeting that included the district program director and the teacher to get the issue resolved.

On his coaching call, his coach listened and witnessed the emotional toll of these types of encounters. His coach asked, "What if you just take a deep breath and let's give the situation some space?" Gary eagerly agreed.

Knowing that building relationships and community in faculty meetings had been a targeted goal for Gary, his coach asked about how his faculty meetings were progressing. Immediately Gary's spirit and voice lifted as he connected with his most recent success. He could hardly wait to share what had happened the day before.

Because the budget process would soon begin, the district had begun to identify harsh staffing cuts. He had been told that he would have to lose a teacher or reorganize to balance his staffing allocation. He knew immediately how to fix the problem: one grade level would have to lose a position. If only one person would volunteer to move, he could make it work. He doubted anyone would volunteer and he would be forced to lose a position.

Because he was committed to openness and honesty with his staff, he decided he would just lay out the options to his staff and let them decide what they wanted to do. At the faculty meeting, he carefully described the situation, even visually listing the three options he thought the school had. He posed questions. What solution did they see as best for students? What was their best thinking? Then he told them, "The solution is yours!"

With intention, Gary, stepped back and watched as they thought and talked through the situation and possible solutions. It was not long before they had agreed that the best option was someone volunteering to move to another grade level. He was beaming at how miraculously they had come to *his* decision. When he asked whom it might be, they requested one week to think and a volunteer would step forward. He was thrilled with his brilliance and how incredibly wonderful it was to watch the process of simply giving them the problem, the facts, and the conditions, and with that information, how easy this difficult decision had been to make.

He was thrilled with his decision to make this process collaborative and for his staff to reinforce how powerful the process was; for it resulted in their ownership, buy-in, and support. His coach celebrated with him that his thinking had resulted in the alignment of his goal for professional collaboration.

His coach then asked him to compare and contrast this situation with the music teacher situation. After a long silence, Gary immediately

*(Continued)*

(Continued)

realized how *his* response resulted in the outcome in both situations. He began instantly to rethink his response with the music teacher and how he could have handled his response so differently. He began to generate his options—he could have said this . . . he could have offered this—all which he now realized would have created a safer environment to examine and assess musical selections while respecting her long history at this school.

He had allowed his attitude toward this teacher to influence his response and recognized he had reacted from his hardwiring—an old mode of authority, of giving approval, and of the one who knows the correct answers. His awareness was rich with insight and perceptiveness.

So his coach asked, "What will you do today to apply this insight?" Immediately his language reflected the energy of multiple options for the upcoming conversations and his intention to be the coach-leader he was striving to be.

## Coaching Insights

With the music teacher, Gary learned that demanding compliance brings more work than it is worth. He let emotions cloud his response, which resulted in making a teacher very angry. In the end, she may most likely comply but it may only be at a superficial level. Once she became argumentative, it would have been better for him to ask for a meeting with the teacher later in the day. This would have given him time to cool down and plan a calmer response.

Gary also learned that he gets better results with his staff when he is not acting as an *expert*, but instead puts himself in the role of the *framer* of the solution—the one who gives facts and conditions as well as *criteria* for solving the problem. Then he lets the people affected by the changes actually figure out how to resolve the problem themselves. This empowers them and puts the responsibility squarely on their shoulders for making the change happen. By doing this, he shows that he trusts his staff's capabilities, which helps them deepen their trust in him.

Our third story is about a principal who feels micromanaged by his district office supervisor. Imagine yourself in a similar position.

## It's in the Details

### Bob Carter

John was principal of an inner city school. In that role, time is a scarce resource. There always seems to be more to do than there is time for doing it.

During one of his coaching sessions, John showed up frustrated and not in a particularly coachable frame of mind. John could hardly wait to share how he was feeling. The district level administrators were trying to micromanage how he should lead the school. Most of them had never set foot on John's campus. Yet, not only were they wrong in some of the things they were expecting him to do, some of what they expected would damage key initiatives that were producing positive results.

John also shared his frustration with staff members who didn't exhibit the level of commitment to excellence he had worked so hard to build. And that's when it happened! As he looked at the situation in his school using the frame he had applied to his supervisors' leadership, he noticed something. And he didn't like what he saw!

From this new perspective, it was obvious. John was trying to micromanage key leaders on *his* staff rather than hold up the standard of a commitment to excellence and empower them to choose how they would do so. While the leadership style of his supervisors was outside his sphere of influence, his own leadership style was not. Immediately, he made a commitment to change his work with staff members. As a result, when he challenged school leaders to make a commitment to excellence, they rose to the occasion. John began to see evidence of excellence immediately!

By holding up a mirror to look at things from a different perspective, John saw details he had not seen before. His coach helped him gain clarity by analyzing one situation and applying it to another.

## Coaching Insights

John figures out a new strategy to use with his staff when he considers a success he has had with a similar issue in the past. Adapting that strategy, he begins to understand that buy-in and commitment comes from the leader showing trust in the capability of his

> By treating people as strong professionals and empowering them to get the desired results, coach-leaders elicit commitment and resolve from the people with whom they work.

staff, setting the criteria and framework for the desired outcome, and then collaborating with staff to determine specific action they can take individually to get the results wanted. By treating people as strong professionals and empowering them to get the desired results, coach-leaders elicit commitment and resolve from the people with whom they work.

The last story tells how one administrator used the strategy of personal coaching conversations to change the climate within a leadership team.

## Change Happens One by One

### Joan Hearne

Chris, an assistant superintendent of a large urban school district, was challenged to move beyond the attitudes of compliance to a genuine buy-in when meeting with a group of district administrators. This leadership group met regularly regarding strategic planning and developing the next steps to be taken in their long-term plan. "The challenge," he shared, "was to continue to build trust and capacity within this diverse group while removing any blocking done by members of the group, both intentionally or unintentionally." Often power struggles would emerge causing either little or no progress, meeting after meeting.

Chris decided to frame with positive intent his desire to increase the engagement and trust in the feeling tone of the meeting. He began to meet individually with several members of the group, one at a time. He chose to start with four people with whom he had the least relationship. His purpose was to share his appreciation for their participation. During each conversation, he noted their increased trust with him. This, in turn, magnified the potential of the total group's influence. Change was beginning to happen one conversation at a time and one person at a time.

After meeting with only four out of the twenty-five members, he noted that each of the four had responded to those personal conversations very positively. They brought this positive tone with them to the meeting with the larger group. He noted that the four were very engaged and that this had helped increase the confident tone of the meeting. With each of the four coming prepared to the meeting, their confidence increased and their willingness to comment during the meeting enhanced the planning and everyone's engagement.

When asked how the meetings were going after several months, Chris shared that focusing on increasing the engagement of a few members instead of trying to change blocking behaviors had paid great dividends. Because of their engagement and advanced preparations, these four members exuded a more positive voice and influence within the leadership team. The trust-building groundwork had begun to change the focus and direction of the entire team to the positive.

The capacity of this team will persist and increase as Chris continues to meet with a few and engage in trust-building conversations with them. The dynamic power of each conversation enhanced and changed the members first and then the whole group. Change definitely happened one conversation at a time.

## Coaching Insights

Often in leadership teams members exhibit competitive and negative behaviors. The paradigm is that if *you* get something, there is less for me. Colleagues certainly don't want to share any vulnerabilities with each other. And if one tells about good things happening at school, colleagues are jealous and complaining rather than happy for each other.

But the trust research is clear. High student achievement can rarely be attained in a climate of low trust. So it is really important that we put the building of trust and rapport high on our priority list within our professional relationships.

Chris knew that he could not counter lack of trust within the group head-on at the meetings. That would likely have only generated blame and complaints. Instead, he used the powerful strategy of having trust-building conversations one person at a time. Rather than focusing on negative behaviors and blocking barriers, Chris chose to get individual buy-in of his leadership team members.

By building trust with the individual members, Chris helped each person feel his trust and support of them as individual members of the team. By sharing his goals and vision for the group, he was able to articulate a new paradigm—a new way of being—for the group. He called them to be their "better selves" and they showed up that way! Chris built on members' strengths and modeled authentic sharing among team members. This impacted the behavior of the entire group.

### Key Ideas for Getting Genuine Buy-In

- Find valuable nuggets of truth by considering past situations which were similar.
  - What made that situation successful or not?
  - If you had been a participant in that situation, what would you have liked the leader to do?
- Trust your staff and treat them as if you truly believe in their capacity.
- Be clear about the desired outcomes.
- Collaborate; don't dictate.
  - Share information and criteria for solutions. Let staff determine the details to get there.
  - Empower those responsible for the change to determine the details of "how-to-do-it."
- Listen to the issues raised by the people implementing the change.
  - Be respectful of legitimate concerns raised.
  - Once a solution pathway is chosen, push for specific action steps.

## Your Learning

1. Which parts of these stories resonate with you? Why?

2. In what areas do you want to strengthen buy-in from others?

3. What could be a useful way for you to reframe thinking to obtain desired support from others?

# Engaging in Difficult
# Conversations

*Most conversations are simply monologues delivered in the presence of a witness.*

—Margaret Millar

Why are some conversations so difficult to have? We know we have to have them, but we avoid them because they take "too much time," or we are afraid of upsetting the "current calm," or we fear the "repercussions." Often, we avoid them because the topic is about an issue that is very important to us. The topic is *personal* for us because we have strong core beliefs and emotions around it. Talking to another person about the topic makes us uncomfortable because we are exposing our deeply held values and we feel vulnerable. We wonder if the conversation will just make us look like raving idiots and we worry that we could lose any power we might have had in making a positive change in the situation. Examples might be talking with a teacher about the subtle racism of her holding low expectations for students from the projects *or* asking a colleague to stop the sexual innuendos in the banter at professional meetings.

Other times we fear the discussion will end up being confrontational and hurt the relationship we have with the other person. We believe the other person is good, means well, and is a friend. And yet, as school leaders, we are responsible for addressing deficiencies and problem areas, especially when they involve the potential for students to succeed. We wonder if the conversation will end up with us sounding like a know-it-all and creating a rift in our friendship.

So how do you start a challenging conversation? Using the reflective feedback steps, as described in David Perkins' (2003) book, *King Arthur's Round Table,* can be a very useful tool to help you get that difficult conversation started. As discussed in Chapter 1, the best kind of feedback takes one of three forms: asking clarifying questions, stating the value potential of the topic or the person, and asking questions that get the other person thinking about possibilities. When these three feedback forms are put together, they make a great frame for starting a difficult conversation. Gina Marx, one of our colleagues, calls this the "CVP frame" for Clarify-Value-Possibility.

Here is how it works. First, be clear about what you want to talk about—*clarify.* Next, name the strengths you see that the other person brings to the situation—*value.* Then ask a question that gets the other person thinking about how they can apply their strengths to the situation—*possibility.* And say all that in about *one minute*! You want to spend your time *listening* to the other person, *not talking at* him or her or *justifying* your position.

> The CVP frame works best when there is a trust relationship and feelings of positive intent between the two people.

The CVP frame works best when there is a trust relationship and feelings of positive intent between the two people, and when the person initiating the conversation is authentic and speaks from the heart.

During the conversation, use paraphrasing and gentle probing skills to gain greater clarity and understanding of the other person's point of view. Acknowledge the position of the other person and express your concerns/issues without using sarcasm, blame, or emotionally loaded language.

At the end of the conversation, identify areas of agreement and difference (if there are any). Then agree on next steps and determine how to hold each other accountable for taking action.

Now let's see how Ratna, a new principal at a middle school, used this tool very effectively to have some fierce conversations with a few of her staff members.

## Moving Staff Up or Out

### Marceta Fleming Reilly

Ratna was a first-year principal in a very challenging school. Her middle school was in "corrective action" because students had not made adequate yearly progress (AYP) two years in a row. The scores were *close*, but they had not made AYP because of one subpopulation in reading and two subpopulations in math. Ratna was focused, urgent, and passionate about achieving student success, and she knew it would take *team* effort to do it.

By February of the school year, Ratna still had faculty members who were not getting positive results with students. Several key teams (math, reading, and special education) seemed cynical and joking that they just needed "better quality kids" to get the results they wanted.

Ratna was very frustrated. She knew the school could not be successful in teaching *all* the students until faculty teams believed it was possible to get good results from the students in *this* school. She was determined that unless team leaders could give their *hearts* to this work, she wanted them gone. It was time for some fierce conversations.

She set up individual meetings with each team leader and used the CVP frame to plan them. She was clear about what she wanted—her vision—for the school: *true belief* in the potential of the students, *commitment to collaboration* among staff and with the community they served, and *full heart* in delivering the best instruction possible for every student.

She took time to clearly identify for herself what the specific issue was for each person with whom she needed to speak. For one team leader, it was superficial collaboration within the team. For another, it was lack of energy and effort in the classroom and doing the minimum required by contract. And for another, it was sarcastic language used with other staff about the ability of certain students to learn. Knowing that what you complain about gives clues to what you care about, Ratna turned each of her complaint situations into something *she* cared about: productive collaboration, enthusiasm about teaching, caring about students.

Then she thought carefully about what she could *authentically* say were strengths in each person with whom she would be talking. She

*(Continued)*

(Continued)

paired that with a "possibility" question that could draw the other person into the conversation while reducing their feelings of defensiveness.

"I believe that productive collaboration in our faculty teams is essential to our school's success. (C) You are very well organized for the team meetings and you are always good with details like getting reports and information to our office on time. (V) What are ways you could use those skills of efficiency and attention to detail to move your team into deeper discussions around the student data your team is collecting? (P)"

"Let's talk about the joy of teaching. (C) You have great knowledge about your course content and you have high expectations for learning. (V) Yet when you are teaching, it doesn't always seem like your heart is into it. So what are things you intentionally plan in your instruction that draw students in and transmit not only knowledge but also enthusiasm about the subject area? (P)"

"To be successful in turning this school around, it is important that we show the community that we truly care about all the students in our school. (C) I have noticed that you are really good at relating to quirky kids—the shy, the late bloomers, those considered geeks. (V) How could you apply the kinds of relational skills you use with them to engage students who are boisterous and more assertive? (P)"

Ratna had these conversations and more. Each was successful, with four staff members making positive changes and one person requesting a transfer to another school.

## Coaching Insights

It takes time and courage to have these kinds of conversations. They are most successful when there is already an environment of trust between the two people in the conversation. Ratna got clear about her issue with each person, thought carefully about the strengths each brought to the school team, and formulated a beginning question that helped the person apply his or her strength to the situation. These steps are the ones that take the *time*—thinking time before the conversation.

During the conversation, she listened and spoke with an open heart. This is the part that takes *courage*. She opened herself to criticism and the possibility of angry confrontation. But because she was known as a principal who was respectful and caring, her sincere listening and demeanor communicated that her concern was about the *issue*, not the *person*.

The next story shows how you can use reflective questions not just for difficult conversations, but also for important conversations— even with yourself!

## Reflection: A Closer Look

### Joan Hearne

In a new position, Scott was responsible for a state-funded student assistance program in a large, urban district. This program provided needed tutoring to many at-risk students in after-school settings during the year. Although this program was not new, the intricacies of setting it up were very complex. With very little support from within his department, he began the school year feeling unqualified and with many loose ends as the program was launched.

Not only did Scott have to learn the program, his department did not allocate any technical assistance for the many tasks at hand. During frequent conversations with supervisors and staff, the complexity of this very large project became clearer. The children were selected through an application process and then parents were notified. Next, principals were informed, the tutoring agencies were contacted, and finally the teachers hired for this after-school program.

Scott discovered he needed to fully understand this state-supported program and its very complex intricacies. So he sought to clarify his role by asking reflective questions of himself and others. He grappled with

*(Continued)*

(Continued)

the enormity of the task and learned much as he answered his own questions.

Before coaching, Scott seldom reflected on the positives and challenges he faced. But after developing good listening and questioning skills, he found that taking time for reflection was extremely valuable. He said it allowed him time to think deeper and to consider if what he was doing made sense or not. He said, "I had time to figure out my own problems rather than listen to someone tell me what to do." Now he is no longer so quick to offer solutions to others; he just asks deeper questions of them.

Throughout his first year in this position, Scott grew in his understanding of the program and its complexity. Within the first year, he had put into place evaluation pieces, upgrades, and streamlined the process for the next year. In a recent conversation, he shared, "I am now more qualified than I thought I was to do what I am doing."

Asking clarifying questions gets the conversation going. By reflecting on the process, he better understood his own practices and then developed other practices that more appropriately reflected the intent of the program.

He learned that there is potential power in every conversation. Even when the conversation was with himself!

## Coaching Insights

Scott used his coach as a thinking partner. His coach would ask a clarifying question and Scott would take it deeper by asking himself a reflective question. As they played off each other, Scott learned what he needed to know and then researched and asked questions of others to find more answers. In the reflective feedback process, Scott grappled with the complexity of his program and sought ways to create greater value and deeper impact for it. He also learned there is great value in taking time to reflect, finding answers for himself. In the end, it accelerated his productivity and effectiveness.

Now let's look at more stories from our colleagues that show other ways to address the issue of having difficult conversations, especially with challenging staff.

## A Marginal Teacher Spurs the Evolution
## of a Coach-Leader

### Gina Marx

Stacy was one of the sharpest principals I have ever known. She amazed me with her quick problem-solving ability, and how she was constantly in the classroom and knew the content and standards she expected from her staff. She was bright beyond belief.

She was also quick to point out her ineffective teachers and how poorly they performed. She would share conversations she'd had with one particular marginal teacher; conversations that were laced with words such as, "I told her she needed to . . ." and "I told her you don't do this with kids . . ." and so on.

But Stacy's quick conversational fixes for this teacher were not producing any noticeable difference with the teacher's performance in the classroom. Stacy was almost feeling as if she needed to write out the lesson plans for the teacher. However, she did express that the teacher loved the children and seemed to really care for them.

Stacy got excited as she learned about positive intent and powerful questioning as coach-leader skills. She practiced with me in preparation for future conversations with this teacher whom she felt was her "biggest problem." At first, she felt like this positive intent stuff might just be thinly veiled criticism. Yet, she discussed the positive attributes of this teacher and felt that she could really believe certain things about the teacher. "I do truly believe she cares about the children," Stacy said.

Stacy was so proud of herself when she reported what she said to the teacher: "Jane, you care deeply about the children in your math classes. I know you want them to do well on the upcoming state assessments. So, with that in mind, what are some things you've been thinking about recently that you might change in your instruction to assure a high level of understanding in the kids?"

The difference in how the teacher responded to this type of questioning was amazing to Stacy. The teacher was open and Stacy felt that the conversation was very productive. The teacher was offering new insights about her own instruction!

Over the course of the next year, Stacy had many coaching conversations with her teachers as well as with this particular marginal

*(Continued)*

(Continued)

teacher who was on a plan of improvement. She felt less nervous going into the conversations as her coaching language skills developed and the teachers were making great progress.

Stacy became exceptionally good at reflective feedback. After walk-throughs, she would go to her office and send e-mails to the teachers she observed. She would pose questions to them, always practicing use of her coaching language. Doing it by e-mail gave teachers time to think more deeply about their responses. Stacy kept these messages in an electronic file for each teacher. When she received their responses to the questions she had posed, Stacy would cut and paste them in the computer file beside the questions she had asked. In this way, Stacy was able to look at her file throughout the year and see the evolution of her coaching language. She delighted in how much she had improved. Best of all, she could see the growth in her teachers because of her emerging coach-leader qualities!

## Coaching Insights

In this story, Stacy learned that positive intent was an important way to *be* with staff. She learned it is communicated not just by the *words* one chooses, but also must be based on a true belief in the abilities and good intentions of the other person. If true belief is not present, the words will feel manipulative to the receiver. The added benefit of positive intent is that when staff members know you are looking for the good things they do and recognize the strengths they have, they are more willing to make changes you request.

Stacy also modeled well for her staff the value of continuous growth. Even though she was an expert in curriculum and instruc-tion, she still wanted to strengthen her skillfulness in using coach-like language. This communicated that *everyone* in the school was expected to grow and learn continuously.

She *frequently* and *consistently* practiced her language as she asked teachers questions through e-mail after observations. She kept records of her language and monitored it over time. This helped her see how communicating positive intent in her language with staff members could very effectively influence the growth of teachers.

In the next story, Kathy Kee tells how one principal tackled a difficult employee and also impacted systemic change.

## Facing Our Dragons

### Kathy Kee

Principal Dan called with an urgent issue: how to best write up and terminate his current secretary.

While experienced as an elementary principal, Dan began his first year at an intermediate school with thousands of areas demanding his attention—getting into classrooms, increasing highly engaging instruction, creating numerous processes and procedures, and building relationships with this new staff who were not terribly open to welcoming this former elementary principal. So little time, so many demands. His secretary, while very efficient, had a reputation of not being kind or caring; she simply was "not a nice person." She was directive and sharp and certainly not the example of what he wanted in the front office. Other than a couple of short conversations requesting specific things from her, he really had avoided confronting the larger issue of her actions and behaviors toward others. On this particular day, she had screamed at an aide for getting into the supply closet, verbally assaulted her using profanity, and demeaned her at such a level that the aide came to the principal with the intention of filing a grievance.

Dan listened fully to the aide and felt embarrassed that he had not dealt with his secretary earlier. He requested that the aide allow him to investigate the incident and get back to her before she did anything. During his investigation when he questioned those who had witnessed the event, no one was willing to provide information. One person even stated she did not want any trouble with the secretary. Dan realized the extent of her influence of intimidation and negative authority.

In a conversation with his coach, Dan asked for assistance with thinking through his next steps and preparing for the conversation to terminate the secretary. Immediately, he admitted he was partly to blame because he knew she was not a nice person and he had avoided dealing with her. Their conversations had focused on their working relationship, and she had responded to all his requests concerning paper work, maintaining the calendar, meeting deadlines, even helping him keep order with all the paper on his desk. He even tackled a conversation with her around secrets. He had stated his expectation was that his

*(Continued)*

(Continued)

secretary keep him informed, not be a gatekeeper of information, be open about things going on, and not be afraid to talk with him. She had always made the effort to do what he asked. With this new issue, his big concern was after presenting the information and facts, long overdue, she would lie or say it was blown out of proportion.

Dan's coach offered that when approached and asked to do things in a certain way, his secretary had complied. Dan began to think about her strengths and he was reconnecting to how organized she was; how efficiently she completed certain job assignments; how she delegated with the office staff to meet deadlines; and how she protected his time on his calendar. He even remembered a funny incident in his office where she became bossy with him about his desk and how they laughed about it.

Dan recognized his fingerprints were all over this situation because of waiting so long to deal with it AND there was so much at stake. He wanted to be a coach-leader by being respectful and supportive in his interactions with this new staff. But in this situation, it was critical that his right hand—his secretary, his administrative assistant—be an example of his values and beliefs in the front office. He knew if he were not willing to hold her to a high standard, how could he ask the same of his teachers and students?

Soon he was preparing his next steps and his conversation with his secretary. Dan wanted to talk with two more people to demonstrate his intention to gather the facts of what happened. He felt this would also send the rippling message through the grapevine that he was "doing something." And then he wanted to sit down and think about the things he valued in his secretary. Dan paused and then said, "You know, she is a good secretary . . . it's just the attitude and outlook." As he considered what he would say to her, he thought. He wanted to affirm her value to the position and what he needed in the position. Dan wanted to express to her some of the great skills she had and how important those had been to him this year. He wanted to thank her for the many things they had accomplished and he wanted to apologize for not talking to her about this before. But there must be a change in her as they went forward. It was important to tell her he needed her efficiency and skills AND *he also needed her to represent him in the front office.* He needed her to be kind, patient, and positive in her dealings with others and most importantly, to be respectful of others.

Dan realized deeply *what was at stake*—a culture of respect and trust was essential for the improvement of this school. If, as principal, he failed to hold everyone to the same high standards and expectations, everything he was attempting to build would be meaningless. He scheduled a time immediately for their conversation.

In the next call with his coach, Dan celebrated his success and it was not the success one might have expected. After his interviews and sharing the facts with his secretary, he offered his secretary the opportunity to take responsibility for her actions and behaviors. Instead of owning up to the behaviors, she denied and blamed others for the situation. Dan had made the decision that he would keep or dismiss her based on her actions in this critical conversation.

Based on her behaviors, he respectfully informed her that she was being removed from her position. She could resign or be dismissed. Once she realized this was really happening, she said all the things he had hoped for in her first response. He told her she had many skills and he wished the best for her, but he needed someone who shared his values and goals as that person represents him in the front office. Without trust and honesty, it was not she. She quietly turned in her keys, gathered her personal belongings, and left.

How courageous this principal had been! This principal, this coach-leader, courageously spoke and listened as if this would be the most important conversation he would ever have. A life and a school were changed as a result.

## Coaching Insights

Dan used Susan Scott's (2004) Confrontational Model to frame his conversation with his secretary (p. 254). His opening statement to her had seven basic steps—all said in one minute or less.

1. Name the issue.

2. Select a specific example that illustrates the behavior or situation you want to change.

3. Describe your emotions about this issue.

4. Clarify what is at stake.

5. Identify your contribution to this problem.

6. Indicate your wish to resolve the issue.

7. Invite your partner to respond.

Then he spent time *listening* to the secretary and digging for full understanding.

Before the conversation began, Dan did a lot of preplanning. He carefully thought through his frame for opening the conversation. He was clear about what action he wanted to see from the secretary. He worked to leave his negative emotions outside the office and took a risk to approach the conversation with openness and trust toward his secretary.

Dan was very clear about his priority values: trust and honesty. When the secretary could not display these vital characteristics to him in a critical, private conversation, he knew he had to dismiss her.

These kinds of difficult conversations are never easy to have. But good frames can help you open the conversation without immediately igniting defensiveness. Then, it takes deep listening and clear knowledge of what is needed for resolution to determine how to move forward.

---

### Key Ideas for Engaging in Difficult Conversations

- Consider using a "difficult conversation" frame to help you start the conversation.
  - ○ The CVP (Clarify-Value-Possibility) is good for important and serious topics.
  - ○ Susan Scott's Confrontation Model is helpful when addressing very challenging behaviors.
- Approach the person with authentic positive intent, then speak from the heart.
- Get clear about the issue you want to discuss and name it.
- Identify the value you see in the other person or the value of the topic of discussion.
- Ask a reflective question that opens possibility thinking.
- Leave the majority of the talk time for the other person and *really listen*.
- Dig for greater clarity and understanding, avoiding negative emotions, sarcasm, and blame at all costs!
- Describe your contribution to the problem and indicate your wish to resolve the issue.
- Frame solution options.
- Acknowledge the other person's position, identifying areas of agreement and difference.
- Together agree on next steps and determine how to hold each other accountable.

## Your Learning

1. Which parts of these stories resonate with you? Why?

2. What conversation have you been avoiding?

3. What coach-like skills will you utilize in planning this difficult conversation?

4. How will you start the conversation so it becomes a genuine dialogue?

_____

_____

_____

_____

_____

_____

_____

_____

_____

_____

_____

_____

# Changing Blamers
# Into Believers

*Underneath the surface torrent of complaints, cynical
humor, and eye-rolling, there is a hidden river of passion and commitment which is the reason the complaints
even exist.*

—Robert Kegan

We have all met our share of whiners, skeptics, and "subver-
sives" on our faculties. We bring a change idea to our school
or district. Despite the research and the possibility it holds for solution to a problem our students are having, somebody is always ready
to punch holes in the idea or dismiss it without even giving it a
chance. *It will be too hard for our kids*, or *Our parents won't support
it*, or *It will take too much prep time when my plate is already over-
loaded with teaching responsibilities*, or *It is just coddling the kids!*

As a new principal in a school with a veteran staff, I (Marceta)
vividly remember being especially concerned about the coddling
complaint. My leadership style was not like that of the previous
principal, and I worked with students and parents differently. So one
of my biggest challenges was creating a student discipline climate
with which I could live.

## Softening Discipline at the Edges

### Marceta Fleming Reilly

The teachers at my new school often sent me misbehaving students from their classrooms and wanted me to "string them up by their thumbs." Teachers frequently waited until the classroom situation was intolerable for them, and then wanted me to support them by dishing out a strict punishment—time-out room, in or out of school suspension, calling parents, referral to district or county services.

I, on the other hand, wanted to hear the student's side of the story as well as the teacher's. The student and I would have a conversation about how things *could have* gone differently. We would role-play different, more socially acceptable responses and discuss better ways to act in the classroom the next time the child's anger or frustration was triggered by someone or something. Sometimes we would call the parent to inform them of the new behavior the child would be practicing and to request their support. The child would leave my office calmer but not *punished*.

The staff was abuzz with my discipline tactics. What good would it do to send students to the office if the principal just talked to them? Discipline would become a joke among students at this school and misbehavior would become rampant! My ears were burning with blame and staff agitation was brewing just below the surface.

I recognized immediately that I had not explained my discipline expectations to staff. I also recognized that their complaints were telling me they valued their teaching time and did not want discipline distractions to interfere with the learning of other, diligent students.

So I called a hasty faculty meeting and explained my preferred way to work with misbehaving children. I explained the results I had had at other schools with this approach, and I assured them we all wanted the same thing—changed behavior in disruptive students. I acknowledged the fact that they valued their teaching time and did not want to have to deal with difficult discipline issues when it took away from students who really wanted to learn.

I solicited volunteers from the staff to meet with me over the next couple of weeks to create discipline procedures that were open and understood by everyone. Teachers should have guidelines for when to send students to the office. The principal should be consistent and clarify for teachers what will likely happen when a child is sent to the office—both during and after the episode.

Fear about impending mass chaos due to "riotous" students subsided. Teachers felt heard and a new, better discipline process emerged because both sides collaborated to develop its detail.

## Coaching Insights

How were my actions coach-like? I listened and was intentional about being respectful when hearing staff complaints about my discipline. I wanted to take it personally and blame them for being so archaic in their approach to controlling students. But deep down, I knew I had to share some of the blame because I had not been clear about my philosophy of office discipline. Staff members did not know what to expect from me and came with a different discipline paradigm in their heads.

I recognized I had a strong, veteran staff. It was important for me to understand their point of view. These complaints were an opportunity to look into the window of their collective values and hold them up for view. Doing that, we found we were more alike than different in what we wanted.

Finally, I worked collaboratively with staff members to develop new norms and expectations for office discipline. I presented the staff with a new framework for discipline and asked them to suggest various actions within that frame—actions that would ensure they felt supported and affirmed when they sent students to me. The key to success for all of us was seeing fewer misbehaving students and students using more appropriate responses in the classroom when they were frustrated or angry. Everybody was responsible for communicating to the group those successes and concerns we observed after students had an office referral.

Our next story is about a teacher who blames the school board and community for what she feels is a bad administrative decision. As you read it, think about situations in which you have opportunities to change blamers into supporters.

## Caught in the Middle

### Reba Schumacher

When Derek came to the coaching call his usually upbeat, cheery greeting was somber and heavy. His own reflection was that he was worried and nervous. He continued by discussing that Nicole, a talented and dedicated teacher on his staff, had become embroiled in a school board and administrative decision. Nicole didn't agree with the decision and for the past two weeks had been attempting to garner support among district staff as well as community members. Not wanting to draw negative attention to herself, Nicole had attempted (sometimes successfully and sometimes unsuccessfully) to recruit others to speak out against the decision through letters to the editor and addressing the school board at their meetings. Nicole had even aligned herself with a particularly negative school board candidate who had a personal vendetta against district administrators.

Derek knew that Nicole was often passionate and influential in the community because of her reputation as a competent teacher. Crossing Nicole could prove disastrous. Not doing so could also have negative consequences for the typically cohesive district.

Derek had been directed by more than one of his supervisors to conference with Nicole and issue a written reprimand for unprofessional behavior. Teachers across the district were complaining that Nicole was attempting to coerce them to speak out against the board and administrators. Additionally, she had failed to follow district process for lodging a complaint. Derek was caught in the middle—feeling compelled on one hand to follow directives and knowing on the other that doing so could cause the seemingly minor issue to reverberate through the community with an unjustified force. He reiterated that Nicole was influential and would not hesitate to use her influence.

Derek wanted to react as a coach-leader. He reflected on how he wanted to *be* with Nicole, so he decided to have a coaching conversation. He elaborated that he saw this as a time to provide feedback, and a conversation involving reflective feedback seemed to be best in this situation.

Derek then spent time hammering out that he wanted to do: Step 1—ask clarifying questions; Step 2—value Nicole's effectiveness as a teacher; Step 3—expand Nicole's awareness through reflective questions. Knowing that clarifying questions must come from a place of sincere, naïve curiosity, he decided to ask if Nicole often felt decisions were made demonstrating a lack of regard for teachers. Step 2 was easy, considering Nicole's competence. He would acknowledge Nicole's dedication to every child's success on the high-stakes accountability test and further personalize his appreciation by recognizing how exhausted Nicole must be with testing just around the corner. His third and final step was reflective: "Are your responses to the board's decision in alignment with your legacy as an educator?" As it was his goal to be intentional and avoid appearing evaluative or judgmental, Derek took a few minutes to practice the conversation.

Suddenly Derek noticed that his nervous feeling had left to be replaced with a sense of calm. He recognized that the use of reflective feedback allowed him to feel in alignment with his leadership style—one of coach-leader. He remembered the few occasions he'd reacted as others decreed; the outcomes had been devastating to him as well as recipient staff. He now had a plan aligned to his core beliefs.

Within days, Derek called his coach and he was back to his normal calm, confident self. The conversation had been a complete success. Nicole acknowledged that in ten years administrators and board members had never before made a decision that caused her to react negatively. As Derek made his value statements, the dam burst, and Nicole began to sob. She chokingly shared how frightened she was about her students' performance on the upcoming test, and how the board decision had contributed to her feelings of inadequacy. The reflective question mobilized Nicole to offer her input into a solution for the issue.

One reflective, coaching conversation not only maintained the integrity of a leader, it prevented the school's loss of a really good teacher and held together a community.

## Coaching Insights

Derek recognized Nicole's strident actions against the board of education as coming from feelings of frustration and anger about not being treated professionally by them. He hit on a key value for

Nicole when he noted her dedication to children's academic success. All the frustration and anger about feeling overworked and underappreciated came flooding out. Once that wall of pain spilled out, Nicole was able to think constructively about how she wanted to *be* as a respected educator. It allowed her to move from militancy and confrontation to a position of quieter, yet powerful, influence because of her excellent teaching reputation.

Derek listened to Nicole deeply and looked beyond her negative behavior. He presumed positive intent on her part; she was talented and dedicated. Then he used the three steps of reflective feedback to artfully frame his conversation with Nicole—clarify the situation; identify the value Nicole brings to the situation; ask a question that has Nicole thinking about possibility for the future. Approaching the issue using the reflective feedback frame made all the difference in the world in the outcome.

The final story in this chapter is about a student who blames the school system for his frustration and anger.

## "Nobody at This School Gets Me!"

### Frances Shuster

These are the words from a fourth-grade boy that invoked the coach-leader identity and behaviors of Principal Sharon.

This wasn't Trent's first time to be sent to the principal's office for misbehavior. This time, his anger was raging out of control. He stood up and threw a book across the table. Sharon feared he would strike her. He said, "You don't understand me. I'm outta here!" and moved toward the door. Sharon placed herself between Trent and the door and staying calm, said, "I want you to talk to me." Trent started to scream, put his hands on his head and pulled his hair. "You don't understand. Nobody here gets me!"

Because the school secretary heard his screaming through the closed door, she alerted the Crisis Intervention Team members, who were standing at the door ready to physically restrain Trent.

As Sharon heard his plea, "Nobody at this school gets me!" she chose a different response. She thought, *If we don't reach him now, I'm afraid we're going to lose him. He is that mad!* A power struggle promised to be ugly. So instead, she said, "You're right, Trent, but I want to, and I'm trying to. Mind if we sit down and talk about it?" Then she listened as Trent's frustration poured out. His emotions calmed. The moment of rage led to an open and honest conversation between him and his principal, which lasted more than an hour. He felt he knew a lot more than he was being given credit for knowing. So Sharon arranged for him to take some assessments that would show his level of knowledge. He felt his level of intelligence was being overlooked. So she arranged for him to be screened for the gifted program at the school.

Sharon also knew that Trent needed to understand standards and expectations for successful students. She explained those clearly, reminded him that he could choose whether or not he was willing to uphold and abide by those standards, and asked him to think about what he wanted to do. She communicated with his mother and explained this new approach she had chosen to take with Trent, while requesting her support.

He left Sharon's office in a totally different frame of mind. His teachers wondered, "Who is this kid?" He was helpful, working hard—things he hadn't done before. He felt he was being understood because of the committed listening given him by his principal. Previously, he had felt trapped, like a caged person ready to explode. The happiness and cooperation came from feeling the empowerment of being given choices he wanted and needed.

The next day, Trent came to the principal and said he had decided he wanted to stay at the school and take responsibility for living up to the standards and expectations she had clearly set forth.

He took a fifth-grade science assessment, which showed that he actually *did* know that content. A math assessment showed he did not know all that he thought he did. His teacher had been constantly reminding him to show his work in math. After taking the assessment, he realized he needed to do that, rather than think he could do it all in his head. Both assessments gave him and his teachers clear information to go by, rather than just a sense of what he knew and what his teachers thought he knew or what they were missing due to his disruptive behaviors.

*(Continued)*

(Continued)

School staff and parents all became partners in reframing their approach to Trent. Trent became a child who felt empowered. He became more thoughtful and reflective, and he worked diligently to make appropriate and productive choices for himself.

The principal, Sharon, is reflecting on how many past students might have benefitted from this approach. More importantly, she knows that if this approach worked with Trent, it shows promise and possibility for benefitting countless other students in the future.

## Coaching Insights

> Taking complaints seriously and listening for the values underlying the complaints help break down walls of frustration and anger.

As with the other stories in this book, the coaching conversation starts with good listening. Children and adults alike become frustrated and angry when they feel that no one is listening to them. So taking complaints seriously and listening for the values underlying the complaints help break down those walls of frustration and anger.

Then it takes following through on the administrator's part. What difference will your new understanding of the situation make in your actions? In Principal Sharon's case, she did testing and added data to the information the student gave her. This data validated some of what the student said but also gave the student some objective information to help him understand his own responsibilities.

Sharon clarified for Trent the standards and expectations for all students. She helped Trent see that he had choices—the power to follow or not follow these expectations was in his hands. She acknowledged she was powerless to make him do something he did not want to do. So instead of playing the power card, she did the counterintuitive thing and took a risk. She was calling him to be his *better self* and accurately guessing that was the person Trent wanted to *be*. She was using positive intent.

Finally, Sharon helped create a support network for Trent. She enlisted the help of his parents and school staff to begin rooting for Trent. Her positive intent about Trent became contagious and people began looking for the good rather than expecting the bad.

## Key Ideas for Changing Blamers Into Believers

- Face the blamer with positive intent and a desire to listen fully.
- Consider what the blamer tells you and reframe the complaint into what the blamer values or cares about.
- Name the values you see in the complaint and acknowledge the validity in it.
- Identify the strengths of the blamer.
- Ask an open-ended question that helps the blamer think through and articulate a preferred future.
- Share your own values and goals involved in the idea on the table.
- Collaborate about what steps to take to achieve a mutually desired future.
- Identify ways to support each other in making the change.
- Create a support network for the change to happen.
- Periodically monitor how the plan is working and consider what mutual adjustments might be helpful.

## Your Learning

1. Which parts of these stories resonate with you? Why?

2. How do you react when you or your school are criticized?

3. What are some coach-like ways to respond?

# Everyone Is Accountable

*Quality is everyone's responsibility.*

—W. Edwards Deming

How often have you noticed that the best organizers, decision makers and teachers who deal with challenging students well; those that keep commitments in a timely manner; and individuals who handle difficult people with care are often the very people to whom we turn when an issue arises? Leaders—both formally recognized and informal leaders—frequently are asked to take on the responsibilities— *the monkeys*—of others.

However, when you take on responsibilities that rightfully belong to others you are sending everyone in the school community messages. One message may be that you *want* to assume others' work and duties because you care about or feel sorry for them. You also may be signaling unconsciously that you have no responsibilities of your own and have plenty of time to do the work of other people. Perhaps you are letting people know that you are the only person in the school who can solve issues and that everyone else should be dependent on your expertise.

Do you really want to communicate one or more of these messages to others in your school? In *Lead, Follow, or Get Out of the Way*, Robert Ramsey (1999) points out, "Time spent on others' problems is time not spent on leadership functions. Leaders support and empower employees to solve their own problems. They don't solve the problems for them" (p. 84).

Instead, employing coach-leader behaviors of committed listening, paraphrasing, assuming positive intent by asking powerful questions, and engaging in reflective feedback holds people accountable for their own behaviors and solutions and supports their personal and professional growth. According to James Kouzes and Barry Posner (2002),

> To strengthen others, leaders place their constituents, not themselves, at the center of solving critical problems and contributing to key goals. This is not always easy to do; leaders must deliberately back off, so that others can figure out for themselves what needs to be done. (pp. 283–284)

By providing opportunities for others to make decisions and become responsible for their own outcomes, the coach-leader creates a community of trust and encourages people to develop competence and confidence in their own leadership skills.

Here is a story about what happened when I (Linda) took on too many monkeys myself. No wonder I was always staying late and taking work home!

## Monkey Collector

### Linda Gross Cheliotes

My schedule for the day was open, and I left home feeling energized and excited because I planned to use my free time to visit lots of classrooms, talk with students and staff, and get started on reviewing the school's budget for next year.

I had no sooner parked my car when a parent stopped me in the lot to tell me that another student in class had teased her child. I said that I would look into the situation and get back to her later in the day.

As I entered the school's general office, the secretary told me that three teachers had already complained to her that morning about their classroom clocks being inaccurate. I told the secretary I would check with the custodian and get back to the teachers.

Just after I had hung up my coat in my office, one of the cafeteria ladies asked me to talk to their supervisor because they were short on supplies for lunch. I told her, "No problem, I'll talk to the supervisor by 9 a.m."

As I sat down to read the forty-three new e-mails on my computer, a teacher walked into my office to tell me she really was not feeling well and probably should have taken the day off. I reassured her that I would obtain a substitute teacher for her class and arrange coverage of her students until the substitute arrived.

It was 7:45 a.m.; students would not be arriving until 8:30 and I already had accumulated enough tasks to keep me busy until at least noon. How had this happened? Why did I feel my energy slipping, and when would I ever get into the classrooms and be the instructional leader I envisioned?

Suddenly, I looked around my office and saw a dozen monkeys—all looking at me to feed and play with them. I recognized a couple of them. There was the budget monkey and I really did plan to take care of him today. The instructional leadership monkey was hiding in the far corner. She rarely had an opportunity to come out and play. But who were all these other monkeys and why were they in *my* office?

In each of the situations I encountered at the start of my "free" day, I had taken responsibility to investigate, handle, and solve issues that really belonged to others. I had actually taught the members of my school community to hand over their monkeys to me. No wonder I felt drained of energy before the actual school day had begun!

## Coaching Insights

One of my favorite books is *The One Minute Manager Meets the Monkey* (Blanchard, Oncken, & Burrows, 1989). The analogy of a bunch of monkeys in my office, each representing one of the work items I had agreed to do, was both a strong visual and felt like an actual weight on my shoulders. Blanchard and fellow authors describe a monkey as "the next move" (p. 26). By this, they mean that a monkey represents a challenge or job to be handled, and whoever agrees to handle the work gets to carry that monkey on his back.

How often, though, do we take on the work or responsibilities that really belong to others? How often do we take on their monkeys in addition to our rightful obligations?

Let's revisit the four scenarios in this story. When the parent accosted me in the parking lot about an incident involving her child being teased by another student, as the principal, I could have told the parent that I would notify the teacher of the children and that the teacher would get back to the parent. I might have also used positive intent and asked the parent what the teacher had said to the mother about the incident. In other words, it would be clear to the parent that the best solution would involve a contact with the teacher rather than entailing an investigation by the principal as a first step.

In the second scene, instead of the principal contacting the custodian, I might again have used positive intent by asking the school secretary what the custodian had told the secretary he was going to do about synchronizing the classroom clocks. I could then ask the secretary to follow through with notifying the teachers.

When the lunchroom employee asked me to speak to the lunch supervisor about low supplies, I might have held a short coaching conversation with her. "Since you know what supplies are essential and missing [a positive presupposition], what are your plans for getting what you need from central supply before our first lunch period?" This assumes positive intent, asks an open-ended question, and provides space for silent reflection. This short conversation sends the message that the lunchroom worker is competent and empowered to develop a solution.

Now, let's review the situation in which a sick teacher must go home, a substitute must be called to replace her, and the students need supervision until the substitute arrives. In such a circumstance, as the principal I was just the right person to oversee the process, yet I did not need to undertake all the work directly. The school already had a procedure for obtaining substitute teachers, and now that I knew a teacher was sick, I could have set that process in motion. I would check the master schedule to see which teachers did not have a homeroom and first period class and then ask the secretary to notify one of those teachers to cover the class until the substitute arrived. At this point, I would have been free to check how the sick teacher would get home or to the doctor's office. I also would have had all of the remaining morning to be the instructional leader I wanted to be.

This final situation demonstrates that coaching conversations are not appropriate for all circumstances. However, the principal could still approach the issue as a coach-leader by listening to the sick teacher, following procedures already in place, and calmly enlisting the help of others rather than trying to handle all of the details, including supervising the students, by herself. The message to all involved is *I am listening, I care, I understand what needs to be done, and I know I can count on your support and expertise.*

In the next story, you will learn how one coach-leader began the process of handing over responsibilities to their rightful owners.

## Whose Problem—Whose Solution?

### Sandee Crowther

Joyce was a new principal at an elementary school. She was pleased that her staff members were so willing to share what was on their minds and seek out her advice for struggles they were having both at school and in their personal lives. She felt "needed" and trusted by her staff. On the other hand, this was consuming a great deal of her time and often caused her to own *their* problems.

She herself was being coached on a regular basis, so she was beginning to see value in the importance of committed listening and helping her staff to clarify their thoughts by asking powerful questions. She was aware of the importance of not giving advice and letting the other person come to a solution, but she was not sure how to do this.

By discussing this challenge with her coach, she identified ways to help her staff develop personal responsibility. She wanted to begin practicing using reflective feedback. She would first ask a clarifying question to help her find out what the individual was really thinking. Was the person concerned about something that had happened or an idea to pursue? It could be as simple as saying, "What is uppermost on your mind?" Joyce would then make a statement to indicate that the person had value or that the idea had value potential. For example,

*(Continued)*

(Continued)

"You have evidence that this is causing concerns for you and your team." The next step would be to ask a question to explore possibilities: "I wonder what would happen if...?" or "What strategies are you considering?"

As Joyce practiced these steps, she realized that she was throwing the topic back to the person who had come to her rather than trying to own it herself and give advice. At first, these steps were sometimes awkward for Joyce, but as she began using questions incorporating the language she heard, new thinking started to occur for the person who came to her with an issue. Over time, Joyce realized the importance of showing value for the person and the importance of opening up to many possibilities, not just one solution.

Some staff members who came to Joyce just wanted to vent and let off steam. In those cases, she learned to "witness the struggle" and remain silent. Often that was all they needed. Some staff members still wanted the quick, easy answer and to be helped with their problems, but over time, Joyce realized that by avoiding giving solutions, she was building the capacity in their own thinking and helping them use their own resources.

## Coaching Insights

Joyce valued the trust and teaming that was developing in her school. At the same time, she recognized that she was spending a great deal of her time doing the work of others. Instead, she decided to practice *not* giving advice to her staff. She focused on committed listening and asking powerful, open-ended questions that resulted in teachers reflecting on their practices and coming up with their own solutions to challenges. By providing reflective feedback that clarified others' thinking and expressing the value or value potential of their plans, staff members ultimately developed their own capacity to be thinkers and leaders.

The next story demonstrates the effects taking on others' monkeys can have on you as a coach-leader. It also illustrates that old habits can be replaced by new, positive habits.

### Just Call Me Mom

#### Linda Gross Cheliotes

Maria had been principal of her school for more than five years when she signed up to be coached. Her school was noted as a top performer on state tests of achievement even though it was a Title 1 school. During her first coaching session, Maria mentioned that she was recovering from a serious illness, yet she spent little time at home with her family and relaxing because she was so busy with work.

When her coach asked, "What kinds of activities fill your day at work?" Maria responded that she was constantly meeting with teachers and parents, found it necessary to follow up on every project in the school, and was overwhelmed with staff requests for help. Then Maria recalled several very specific examples of ways she was intimately involved in teacher projects. Maria even remembered the words she had used when the staff members had first approached her about these projects. Each time Maria responded to staff requests for assistance or had an issue to discuss, she usually said, "What can *I* do to help you?" or "How can *we* work on this together?" Through reflection, Maria suddenly had an important "aha" moment of insight. "I keep asking my staff members how they want me to help them and of course, they then assign me work to do!"

Next, she thought about where else these words showed up in her life, and Maria immediately realized it was when she was home interacting with her children. Maria had carried over her home role as mom into her professional life. She had *taught* her staff to think of her as their *mom*—always ready to help and even take on projects that really were the responsibility of staff members. "Oh no," she exclaimed, "I want staff members to know that I care and support them, but I really do not want to be their mom!"

For the next several months, Maria practiced a new way of being with her staff. She was as caring and supportive as she had always been, but she was very intentional about how she spoke with teachers and other staff members. She practiced asking them open-ended questions,

*(Continued)*

(Continued)

beginning with positive presuppositions. For example, when the school guidance counselor organized a food collection drive, Maria said to him,

> You have developed an important project that will teach our students about caring for others. What are *your* plans for fully engaging the students in this community work so that they will focus on our character development goal of service to others? In addition, we are concentrating on improving math skills in Grades 1–4 this year. What suggestions have the teachers made for integrating this project into their math lessons?

While the guidance counselor did not have an immediate response to Maria's questions, she told him that they would discuss the project again in two days.

## Coaching Insights

As her former self, Maria would have immediately taken the initiative to contact the teachers, help them develop lesson plans related to the community project, and even organize a follow-up assembly for the students to celebrate the success of their food drive.

In her new coach-leader role, Maria was still being supportive, yet she intentionally stepped back so her school's guidance counselor and teachers took responsibility for planning, organizing, and following up on the food drive. As a result, the drive was more successful than it had been in previous years; students were actively engaged in practicing service toward others, and staff members felt a sense of accomplishment in their new leadership roles.

Because Maria was no longer *mom* of her school, her health improved and she had more time to spend on her own professional responsibilities. At the same time, she discovered she could leave work earlier each night and took little or no work home on the weekends. She had much more time to be with her husband and to be mom to her own two children. She even had time to take better care of herself.

The final story in this chapter illustrates how the micromanagement monkey may easily slip into your office or classroom and demonstrates how to send this monkey back to his own home.

## Middle School Under Attack

### Edna Harris

Alan is a district superintendent responsible for the supervision of seventeen school leaders in one feeder pattern of a large suburban school district. One of these leaders, Sarah, is an intelligent, experienced, hard-working individual selected by the district leadership team to open a brand new middle school. This facility had been equipped with the latest in technology and designed to accommodate collaborative learning experiences—a futuristic curriculum vision for the district. Many community members, including the school board, had contributed input into the design of this building.

After the school had been in operation for several months, Alan started receiving e-mails and phone calls from some of Sarah's parents expressing concern about the lack of feedback they were receiving regarding the instructional program designed for their children. When talking with his coach, Alan expressed his frustration regarding this situation. He said that during his upcoming midyear evaluation with Sarah, he was really going to tell her what she needed to do to remedy this situation. The coach reminded him that he had shared what a strong leader he thought Sarah was and that she had been selected to lead this school based upon her demonstrated leadership skills. Then his coach asked Alan what parent notification system Sarah had implemented at her school.

Alan was absolutely speechless! He realized he had only heard the perceptions of a few parents and had assumed that Sarah did not have a plan in place. This insight caused him to totally change his approach to the conference. Rather than tell Sarah what she needed to do, Alan elected to ask her about her parent involvement plan and see what was in the plan that he could support.

By listening to Sarah, he learned that she had created an updated school website and that she maintained a blog to keep parents informed. As he continued to ask questions, Sarah reflected and realized these strategies were both passive and behind the scene. She decided that she wanted to be more visible, open, and approachable to the public.

They discussed several options, and she decided to add two things to her parent information strategies. First, she would set up student-led

*(Continued)*

(Continued)

tours of the school; she could meet and greet the patrons before or after the tour to answer questions. Second, she would schedule some brown bag lunches for parents. Sarah agreed that these strategies would help her meet her new goal to be more visible. Alan left that conference feeling like Sarah and he were now working collaboratively to meet the needs of the students and parents at her school.

Within a few weeks, Sarah had implemented the tours and the parent lunches. When Sarah later expressed confusion about the priorities around the instructional program she had been asked to implement, she called Alan and expressed her concern. He subsequently set up a meeting involving the superintendent, Sarah, and himself. Alan was intentional about his role in this meeting—to support Sarah and to focus the dialogue around communicating instructional programs and strategies to the community.

The conversation with the superintendent and Alan provided the clarity Sarah needed to communicate the instructional program more clearly to her students' parents. Her visibility and openness enabled her to form more collaborative relationships with the parents. Not only did Sarah appreciate the support she had received from two district administrators, the concerned parent calls to Alan's office decreased substantially. This was a win-win for both Sarah and Alan!

While Sarah received the support she needed, Alan had learned the importance of positive presuppositions and allowing another person to think about and take on her own responsibility, which added to her feelings of competence.

---

When we take on the responsibilities and issues to be solved by others, our real message may be that we do not fully trust them to have a good solution or that we know a better way to handle challenges.

## Coaching Insights

One monkey that may slip into your office or classroom is named *Micromanagement*. We may tell ourselves that we are feeding and playing with this monkey because we want to be supportive and helpful to others. However, when we take on the responsibilities and issues to be solved by others, our real message may be that we do not fully trust them to have a good solution or that we know a better way to handle challenges.

Fortunately, in the preceding story, Alan realized before he met with the principal that he was thinking like a micromanager rather than a supportive coach-leader. Instead of asking her why she was not employing specific strategies to engage parents, he asked Sarah open-ended questions about what she was doing to communicate with her school community. This approach provided an opportunity for Sarah to reflect on her current strategies and what other approaches she might use.

Alan also acted as a committed listener and opened the conversation with the positive presupposition that the principal was using a number of effective activities to work with parents. As a result, Sarah felt supported rather than reprimanded. She was reinforced for her leadership skills, which increased her confidence in the job she was doing.

Moreover, a trusting relationship developed between Sarah and the district superintendent because he encouraged her to seek her own solutions for better parent communication and involvement rather than telling her what next steps to take.

---

### Key Ideas to Support Accountability in Others

- Handle just your own monkeys (responsibilities).
- Encourage others to nurture and handle their own responsibilities.
- Listen with commitment when others have challenges that need solutions.
- Presume positive intent that the person has the ability and willingness to develop solutions and plans.
- Ask others open-ended questions that cause deep reflection about the challenges and open up possibilities for solutions.
- Provide support and encouragement for solutions by others through reflective feedback.
- Avoid giving advice to others.

## Your Learning

1. Which parts of these stories resonate with you? Why?

2. How will you now differentiate when situations are your responsibility or those of others?

3. What are you planning to show support without taking on others' responsibilities?

_____

_____

_____

_____

_____

_____

_____

_____

_____

_____

_____

_____

_____

_____

_____

_____

_____

# Balancing Personal and Professional Commitments

*Live with intention. Walk to the edge. Listen hard. Practice wellness. Play with abandon. Laugh. Choose with no regret. Appreciate your friends. Continue to learn.*

*Do what you love. Live as if this is all there is.*

—Mary Anne Radmacher

You were hired for your professional position because one or more people recognized your talents, skills, and knowledge and believed you were the best candidate to handle your job successfully. Perhaps you were looking forward to bigger challenges in your work or thought you could have a greater positive influence on the education and lives of students. Your vision, your hopes, your dreams were so clear to you and you were excited, energized, and passionate about all of the possibilities that lay before you.

Now fast-forward—perhaps a few months, perhaps a few years. What are your feelings about your work now? Has your enthusiasm remained high and your daily energy increased? Or are you feeling tired much of the time, sometimes overwhelmed by paperwork and activities that pull you away from your vision of impacting and helping students achieve at high levels? Have you missed being with your family and friends as much as you used to? You still have your gym membership, but when was the last time you worked out on a regular basis? On a scale from 1 (low) to 10 (high), how much stress are you experiencing at this moment? How typical is this level of stress on a daily basis?

Although all occupations have their challenges and stressors, the field of education is one occupation that touches all people in our society. While each person has his own reasons for becoming an educator, you knew from the start that it would not be a 9-to-5 job or one that was likely to bring you great material wealth. You knew that education would require continuous learning on your part and impact both your professional and personal life. Yet you became an educator and now desire to be a coach-leader in your school community.

But how is it possible to balance your personal desires and challenges with those of your professional life? According to Zig Ziglar (2008), "You can have total success when you balance your physical, mental and spiritual, as well as your personal, family and business life" (p. 106). While this statement makes sense, just how does it translate into your daily life?

> Life is a series of choices and being free from stress is one of them.
>
> —David Zerfoss (2011)

David Zerfoss (2011) emphasizes, "Life is a series of choices and being free from stress is one of them" (p. 6). He goes on to state, "Our purpose is our heart and soul. It's who we are and why we exist. When we are 'on-purpose' we are at our best, we are in the zone; we feel energized. We have meaning. When we are off-purpose, we can become stressed" (p. 95).

So how do you translate these inspirational sayings into being a coach-leader who remains passionate about your work yet maintains balance to enjoy all those personal parts of your life that bring you joy and satisfaction, too?

One of my (Linda) coaching clients had moved halfway across the country to take a position as a school district's director of technology. She had always worked for corporations, and her new position was causing her great stress since her learning curve was so steep.

As you read Nadia's story, notice what she did both to handle her stress at work and to balance time to nurture her newly developed relationships.

## Sitting on a Seesaw

### Linda Gross Cheliotes

Nadia felt comfortable with all aspects of technology, yet she expressed to her coach how inadequate she felt about applying her skills in the field of education. After all, she had never even been a teacher and yet she was supposed to help the entire educational staff of her school district integrate technology into their lessons.

On the other hand, Nadia had begun to develop new friendships both at work and in her new church community. In fact, she was dating a wonderful gentleman from her church yet rarely had quality time to get to know him better, let alone experience the companionship of other women she craved.

Instead, Nadia spent hours reading articles about educational technology, searched countless websites on her computer, and investigated possible workshops she might attend that would support her in her job. She was so busy *doing* things that she had lost sight of how she wanted to *be* as the director of technology.

Once her coach asked her to clarify and simplify her professional goals, Nadia realized that her main focus would be to find out what technology the teachers actually needed or wanted to enhance their teaching. It occurred to Nadia that she had not spoken to a single teacher or observed a single lesson since her arrival in the district. In addition, she had two assistants who had been full-time teachers previously and who could be excellent resources, too.

Nadia was energized and ready for action. She developed plans to meet formally and informally with teachers from various content and grade levels. She scheduled time to discuss technology hardware and software already in place and future needs with her two assistants. Yet something still was missing.

*(Continued)*

(Continued)

Although Nadia was becoming more confident and effective in her professional endeavors, she still was unsatisfied with the time and energy she was allotting to her personal life. She loved to exercise but so far had been skipping her gym classes; she saw promise in her dating relationship, yet lacked the time to spend with her new friend. Nadia also enjoyed the times she spent with women from work and in her neighborhood.

Since Nadia was familiar with Stephen Covey's 1990 work *The 7 Habits of Highly Effective People*, her coach asked what Nadia's plans were to put Covey's Third Habit—"putting first things first" (p. 148) into her personal life.

Immediately, Nadia recognized that just as she had set priorities at work, she wanted to set priorities for personal time, too. She found a girlfriend who also wanted to exercise more, and they supported each other by attending weekly classes together. She set aside time each week devoted strictly to spending time with the new man in her life, and she set up lunch dates with her new-found girlfriends. Nadia even set aside some alone time for reading or just sipping her favorite wine while watching the sunset.

What Nadia had learned was the importance of overall balance in her life to decrease or even eliminate her major sources of stress. She realized she had choices about her activities and had to be *intentional* about her choices. In addition, she learned that balance does not mean that one's life is evenly divided. Just as when children go up and down on a seesaw, sometimes you must devote more time to professional duties, while at other times personal responsibilities and preferences take precedence. It is the choice to create overall balance in one's life that reduces stress.

## Coaching Insights

First, Nadia needed to recognize that her life was out of balance. Once she clearly defined both her professional and personal priorities, she was able to create plans in both arenas that would move her toward her goals in a purposeful manner. In other words, she was *intentional* about how she wanted to *be*—a person with both an enjoyable, constructive profession and a rich personal life filled with engaging friends and purposeful activities.

Does this mean that Nadia no longer experienced stress or that her life was always in perfect balance? Of course not! There were days when Nadia worked long hours or missed her exercise class and spent less time focusing on her new relationships. Overall, however, she felt more in charge of her life because she recognized that she had choices. Sometimes those choices involved periods of imbalance between her professional and personal life. And she also realized that when she felt out of balance, she could choose to reprioritize her time and activities.

Another of my (Linda) clients had mastered the balance between his home and school life. However, Athan's emotional stress and imbalance derived from his interactions with school staff, particularly one cantankerous teacher who always challenged rules and expectations.

## The 180-Degree Turnaround

### Linda Gross Cheliotes

Athan was the math and science department chair in his large high school. In spite of his many work projects, he had carefully carved out rewarding time in his schedule for family and community activities.

At work, however, he was feeling highly stressed and negative—not because of the large amount of work for which he was responsible, but because several teachers constantly complained to him about shortcomings in the curriculum and their students. One teacher in particular, Connie, sent his stress level sky high. Just seeing her in the hallway raised his blood pressure! Athan had observed Connie's classes a number of times and realized the teacher was very disorganized, and her conversations with low-performing students undermined their confidence. Connie had expressed to Athan that these students were incapable of meeting district and state math requirements.

In conversations with his coach, Athan could have gone on for hours discussing Connie's shortcomings. Instead, his coach asked him not just

*(Continued)*

(Continued)

what kind of conversation he wanted to have with Connie, but also how he wanted to *be* in this coaching conversation. Then Athan had an important insight. He was choosing to be stressed and unbalanced when he saw or thought about Connie, and he also could choose not to let Connie get under his skin.

Once Athan had this insight, he intentionally planned a coaching conversation with Connie about both her attitude toward some of her students and her classroom management. In fact, Athan could even recognize some of this teacher's strengths: She knew the curriculum well and worked cooperatively with her department colleagues. She even used effective management strategies with her advanced math class and gave them support and encouragement.

Athan decided to approach his conversation with Connie by using positive intent, focusing on the strengths she had demonstrated with some of her classes. He created a list of open-ended questions and made a personal pledge to listen to her responses with commitment. Athan rehearsed with his coach a possible coaching conversation with the teacher, practicing paraphrasing and reflective feedback along with his other coach-leader skills. He wanted to remain calm during his upcoming conversation with the teacher.

Although Athan recognized that he could not force Connie to change her behavior and negative attitude toward some students, he knew that *he* could choose to make a 180-degree turnaround in how he approached the teacher. This single, major insight decreased his work stress significantly, and he began the process of observing staff with a balanced viewpoint based on real data rather than personal emotion.

## Coaching Insights

Athan's stress and imbalance resulted from his own perceptions, reactions, and behaviors, triggered when he saw or interacted with one particular teacher who did not share his values and goals about all students. Consequently, his neural habit of negativity toward the teacher was reinforced on almost a daily basis. It was not until Athan had the personal insight to recognize that he had a choice about how he reacted to the teacher, that he was able to create an intention to develop a new neural pathway or habit of mind that focused on the positive qualities that the teacher demonstrated.

Once Athan changed his reaction and behaviors 180 degrees, he could then focus on holding coaching conversations with the teacher. He realized that the best way to work with this staff member was to focus intentionally on her positive attributes and utilize the four basic coaching skills of committed listening, paraphrasing, positive intent, and reflective feedback.

At the very least, Athan's stress level was reduced and he would be able to have a balanced viewpoint, supported by unemotional data, to take whatever supervisory steps would be necessary to support the teacher's growth or formulate an exit plan for her. At best, he could work on building a trusting relationship with the teacher and in the process, she might actually adjust her attitude toward her students and develop a more positive classroom management style.

How many times each week do you find yourself wondering how to get all of your responsibilities taken care of, let alone have time to do something for yourself? Balancing relationships, work and home responsibilities, getting enough sleep, staying energized, and maybe finding some time to just daydream are some of the priorities you deal with each day, each week, each month, each year.

In our next story, Howard is a principal who confronts many of the same challenges you do. You will learn about a tool that helps Howard maintain his life balance and, as a consequence, decreases his stress.

## Reframing Balance

### Riva Korashan

How often have you asked yourself the question "How do I balance all of the demands of my work with time at home with my family?" Howard, a principal of an elementary school, was no exception. The pull to have

*(Continued)*

(Continued)

more time at home with his wife and children, including a newborn, was competing with the amount of time he was spending at school keeping up with his paperwork. Taking work home with him wasn't a solution—he was home but not with his family. Howard tried using strategies many of us use—keeping a "to do" list, planning ahead, delegating to others—but they didn't work to any great extent. Howard still had a strong belief that he had to do it all or he wasn't doing his job.

During coaching conversations, Howard reflected on "What is it about not getting it all done that doesn't sit well with me?" This question led Howard to explore the idea of time management from many different perspectives. He identified that he is a perfectionist, wanting to do things right. He also realized that he is a procrastinator and allows urgency to define his priorities rather the importance of the work itself. These realizations prompted another question that Howard asked himself: "How can I prioritize my work in a proactive way?"—a way that places realistic boundaries on my time at school. He came up with the idea of creating a *time budget* that would consider both the amount of time certain tasks took to complete and Howard's number one priority—being visible, present, and available to the teachers in his school.

It was humbling for Howard to admit he had a time management issue. He thought about reframing his problem into something that he wanted—a solution. This led Howard to realize that, for him, time management was a matter of personal integrity. Better management of his time was a way of matching his values as a principal, husband, and father with his actions. His new time budget started with what time each day would begin and end, and then Howard would purposefully plan the time in between that would take into consideration his work priorities—meaningful classroom visits especially, and some time in the afternoon to attend to all that paperwork—while also leaving some wiggle room for the unexpected situations that are part of the life of any school.

Howard acknowledged that coaching around time management was really an opportunity to take a closer look at himself. He was able to examine his values and align them with his actions. He reframed his thinking of time management from a stressor to part of the job that he can now do in a very purposeful and intentional way. Seeing the differ-ence his planning made at work and at home was empowering and a gift he could give to his wife, family, school staff, and himself.

## Coaching Insights

Through working with his coach, Howard recognized that time management was a real challenge in his life. It was difficult for him to admit this because he was a perfectionist who "wanted to do it (his job and personal life) right." By reflecting on his values and priorities, he was able to create a tool—a time budget—that helped him reframe his thinking about use of time without feeling guilty. Instead, he is now very intentional about what he chooses to do and NOT do with his time.

I (Marceta) wrote the final story in this chapter. Just as Nadia, Athan, and Howard learned that they had choices about what they could do to reduce stress and regain life balance, my client, Marlena, also discovered a tool for reducing her stressors.

## Running in Circles

### Marceta Fleming Reilly

Marlena was feeling angry and very stressed! As an assistant principal of a school, she had just finished reviewing the results of an inventory of her leadership practices as rated by her supervisor, two direct reports and one "other" person. The news did not look good to her. Three of the four raters consistently agreed with her rating of herself. But one direct report rated her substantially lower on most measures.

Marlena had worked so hard this year to bring a much-needed focus on teaching and learning to the school. She knew she had made some hard decisions, and she believed that the staff supported her in making these changes. Why couldn't this other person see the value of these changes at the school?

*(Continued)*

(Continued)

Marlena had tried not to take this one person's ratings personally and to just look at it as a piece of information that may or may not have validity based on the rest of the ratings. But she had not been successful with that strategy. It was affecting how she felt among her assistant principal colleagues. At their regular Assistant Principal Fellows meetings, she saw all of her colleagues as talented and brimming with expertise. Now with these rating results, she felt vulnerable and diminished among them. On top of everything else, she had some serious health issues, over which she had no control, that were looming on the horizon.

Marlena was discouraged and her stress levels were off the charts. She was short-tempered with her family and losing sleep over her feelings of insecurity. Her coach reminded her that she did not really know why *Other* rated her as she did. Nor did she really know what the other assistant principals thought about her. And she certainly did not know what results would come from her health tests. All of these things were out of her control.

Marlena thought about Covey's (1990) Circle of Concern (pp. 81–91). Within the outer circle are all the things that we care and worry about. The next circle inside that one is the Circle of Influence. It contains all the things we can *influence*, but don't have the power to control final decisions. In the center is a smaller but very powerful circle. It is the Circle of Focus, containing all the things we directly control. She knew that keeping her focus on that center would help her let go of all the worrisome stuff outside of it.

So Marlena named her worries and concerns and mentally placed them in one of Covey's circles. Within that Circle of Focus she could do the following:

- Review the survey findings with a trusted advisor to get an objective perspective on the results
- Get to work on the presentation she and others were making in the near future at the Assistant Principal Fellows meeting
- Ensure that she watched her diet and exercised regularly in order to prep her body for whatever might come

When Marlena began to focus on the things she could control, she immediately felt relieved and empowered. From this position of strength, she was able let go of the doubts and worries that had plagued her. She felt whole, and not broken or out of control. She was able to change her story about herself and her relationships. She was able to focus on the positive.

## Coaching Insights

Marlena used a tool, Covey's Circle of Influence, to reframe her thinking. This helped her recognize that change began with her—not changing others. In other words, she focused on those things she directly controlled. She also changed the story about herself from being a misunderstood victim to being a person who took control of what she could. Finally, she used positive intent when thinking of other people's actions. This new way of thinking provided her with a sense of positivity that could help both her professional relationships and her own health.

### Key Ideas for Maintaining Life Balance and Reducing Stress

- Clarify your priorities and then schedule and keep these priorities.
- Recognize that there are ups and downs in the patterns of balance in life. Balance *over time* is the desired outcome.
- Realize what people, activities, and situations trigger your stress.
- Create an intention to develop positive habits of mind.
- Talk with trusted friends or family members when stressed.
- Acknowledge that you only have control over your own behavior, thoughts, and emotions.
- Prepare for and hold coaching conversations with individuals who trigger negativity in you.
- Incorporate coach-leader skills in difficult conversations.

## Your Learning

1. Which parts of these stories resonate with you? Why?

2. What strategies are you using when you feel stressed by competing priorities?

3. What coach-like strategies are you thinking of using to interact with individuals who trigger negative reactions within you?

_____

_____

_____

_____

_____

_____

_____

_____

_____

_____

_____

_____

_____

_____

_____

_____

# Navigating Successful Life Transitions

*It's never too late to be what you might have been.*

—George Elliott

Throughout your life, you will make many transitions. As you grow older, you may change habits, move elsewhere, raise children, develop new interests, and even transform your beliefs and friendships.

In your professional career, you may ask for or be assigned a new position, decide to move into a formal leadership role, or think about changing professions. At some point, you may decide to leave your current school district for another, and eventually, you may choose or need to retire.

Life transitions may raise hopes, fears, joy, and stress. As much as we enjoy or dislike our current state and activities, we experience some measure of comfort because we usually know what to expect. The future, however much we plan for it, is full of uncertainty and may result in us wondering if we are making the right choice. Life transitions involve taking a risk—a leap of faith into a new set of possibilities and opportunities.

> Life transitions involve taking a risk—a leap of faith into a new set of possibilities and opportunities.

In the story "Rewiring," Jacob is certain that he wants to retire and spend more time engaged in his favorite pastimes. His worry, though, supported by data and his own observations, leaves him wondering about the timing of his retirement. He is a dedicated leader who wants to leave his school well on the way toward implementing the learning goals expected by the school district. Should he work another six months, another year? Perhaps there is something else he could try that will encourage and support his staff move forward in their strategic learning before he leaves the principalship?

## Rewiring

### Linda Gross Cheliotes

Jacob is a veteran principal in a well-performing suburban school. Even though he is preparing to retire soon, he continues to emphasize his core value to have high expectations for achievement by all students. This value means that Jacob also has very high expectations for the performance of his staff and himself.

As part of the school district's instructional initiatives, all teachers in the school have received training in Professional Learning Communities (PLCs) to foster individualized instruction. Jacob is proud that his teachers know how to read and interpret student achievement data accurately. He has toiled diligently to provide time and space for grade-level colleagues to work together every week.

The challenge Jacob brought to sessions with his coach was how to move his staff to the next level of the PLC process. While his teachers clearly understood the data about their students, this information did not change either the content or the instructional practices they used in their classrooms. The students were still grouped for instruction as they had been at the start of the school year, and most staff members used teacher- rather than learner-directed instructional strategies.

When he reflected more deeply, however, Jacob recognized that one group, the second-grade teachers, actually *had* changed their teaching styles and had begun to provide instruction to students according to individual learning needs that the teachers had gleaned from both their personal observations and their analysis of students' work.

So, why had one group of teachers moved to a higher level of implementation of their PLC training while the rest had not? Jacob committed to ponder this question more and gather data from his informal observations for the following two weeks.

Through further reflection and focused observations, Jacob realized that he had made an important discovery about his own interactions with his staff. Typically, he joined and even led the weekly grade-level meetings. However, Jacob often missed the second-grade teachers' meetings because it was held during the first period of the day on Mondays, when the principal was frequently busy handling a variety of tasks, such as introducing substitute teachers to their classes and having informal conversations with parents and staff members.

Jacob comprehended that in his absence, the second-grade teachers had taken personal responsibility for implementing the PLC strategies they had learned, and their trust in each other grew as they supported their colleagues' efforts to try new grouping patterns and instructional approaches.

With this new knowledge, the principal decided to try some new coach-leader strategies with his other grade-level teams. During a general staff meeting, Jacob announced that he would be attending fewer grade-level meetings and when he was present, his role would be that of a listener and sounding board rather than the leader of the meetings. For the present, he would provide each group with some open-ended, guiding questions, such as "Within your three first-grade classrooms, the data reveal seven students who still have not mastered the concept of one-to-one correspondence. What alternative instructional strategies will you use with these children to guarantee that they learn this important mathematical concept? And how will you know they actually have mastered this concept?"

Although it would be a challenge for Jacob to refrain from running the meetings, he resolved to focus on being a committed listener, avoid giving advice, and instead, paraphrase teacher comments for group clarity.

Over the next two months, Jacob attended fewer and fewer grade-level meetings. At the same time, he observed that the teachers were collaborating more with each other as they planned lessons, and there was additional individualization of instruction for students in each classroom. Jacob also noticed a new positive energy in the school. Teachers were more excited about their work with the children, and they demonstrated greater confidence about sharing their teaching experiences and ideas with their colleagues.

*(Continued)*

(Continued)

Rather than feeling worried about his approaching retirement, Jacob was looking forward to leaving the school's students in the capable hands of their teachers. While Jacob was preparing to retire, he had used his coach-leader skills to help his staff rewire their roles as coach-leaders, too.

## Coaching Insights

Although Jacob was very clear about his vision and expectations for all in his school, his impending retirement forced him to reflect upon very specific instructional strategies he wanted to see staff implement successfully before he would feel comfortable about leaving the school. Jacob first needed to clarify what his staff was or was not doing as they moved forward toward fully implementing individualized instruction through PLCs. Although he first thought none of the grade-level teams were implementing PLCs beyond understanding data collection procedures, by thinking very clearly about each grade, Jacob had an "aha" moment that his second-grade staff had indeed mastered the entire individualized instructional process expected by the school district. By focusing on his positive presumption that if this one grade level was successful the others could be, too, Jacob then moved forward by examining what was different about the second-grade level meetings.

Once the principal realized that the second-grade team had become teacher leaders in his absence, Jacob was ready to plan for a similar result in the remaining grades. He knew that he wanted to *be* supportive of the remaining staff and not leave them feeling adrift on their own. This was a very important personal acknowledgment because Jacob was then able to develop an action plan that gradually turned responsibility and leadership over to his staff. He would attend fewer and fewer of their grade-level meetings and during the meetings he attended, his role would be one of support rather than leader. Jacob also provided some initial, open-ended, guiding questions for the meetings that helped staff focus on using the data they had to plan individualized instruction.

As the teachers took more responsibility and leadership in their meetings, their confidence in themselves and their colleagues grew. So did their mutual trust. Jacob had learned an important lesson, too— that sometimes leadership works best from a distance. Others then have the space and opportunity to develop as coach-leaders, too.

Our second story about successful life transitions describes how an individual recognizes that she is in a position in which she is neither personally happy nor professionally rewarded. Find out how Julia makes a 180-degree transition resulting in her dream job.

## I Feel Like a Failure

### Dayna Richardson

For many years Julia exuded a *can do* attitude as an educator—first as a teacher, then as a teacher leader, and then as an administrator. She worked in several districts, being promoted to roles of leadership in each of these districts, before becoming the assistant principal at a large, urban high school. Along the way she also completed her doctorate, made presentations at national conferences, and implemented two new programs in two districts. During many of our early coaching conversations, she would say, "I feel like a failure because the principal and I are not on the same page. I do not trust her." There were many tears and times she wanted to just quit, feeling she was a failure.

Julia knew she was not happy but did not know what to do. When asked, "What are some possibilities? When you reflect on what gave you happiness in your other positions, what was happening?" energy returned to her voice. She shared that she loved to be a presenter (teacher), she liked working with data, and she loved to write. Once she had a focus of what she LOVED, she began looking for solutions. No longer did she feel like a victim. Julia began looking for other positions, knowing what she wanted and what she did not want. She was offered one position, but she said it did not meet her requirements.

Julia continued to be a dedicated administrator, but her state of being changed from one of a failure to one of joy and openness. She now had a focus and purpose.

*(Continued)*

(Continued)

Several months later, a position in a neighboring district opened that was a perfect fit. She applied for it, interviewed, and was asked to join that leadership team. She is now using all of her skills and loves going to work every day. Once she began focusing on solutions instead of the problems, her dream came true.

## Coaching Insights

How often have you or others you know, expressed how negative you feel going to a job that is not fulfilling? Yes, many people work in positions they do not like because they believe they have no other options and must fulfill their financial and familial responsibilities. Attitude is critical when faced with challenging circumstances such as these. John Maxwell (2002) notes the following:

> If you believe that something is a problem, then it is. However, if you believe that something is merely a temporary setback, an interim obstacle, or a solution in the making, then you don't have a problem . . . It's just a matter of attitude. (p. 137)

In the above story, Julia felt stuck and even a failure in her current position. Through coaching, she transformed her thinking about her job. Instead of focusing on her problem of being in a bad position, she intentionally focused on developing solutions. Notice, Julia did not abruptly quit her job with no plan for the future. Rather, through reflection about what made her happy in her work, she gained clarity about her goals and priorities and developed an organized plan of action that would move her to goal achievement. Her coach listened with commitment and silence but did not give Julia advice about what to do. She provided Julia space for reflection, clarity, and dreaming about other possibilities by asking her open-ended questions; reminding her about all of her talents, skills, and accomplishments (focusing on positive intent!); and giving her opportunities for reflective feedback.

Our final story in this chapter demonstrates how clarity of goals, deep reflection, and intentional planning may not only support one person's life transition but also affect how others think about and plan transitions, too.

## Investing in the Next Steps

### Joan Hearne

Meeting Rosemary in her last year as a curriculum leader in her district was such a privilege. She was on the cutting edge of new research and moved about her district with authority and direction, helping teachers grasp new concepts and investing in their growth. Yet, within a few months she was retiring from her current position and would begin a new journey that was unfocused and without concrete direction. During the next few months, having a coach herself helped provide Rosemary with possibilities, allowed her to create her own vision, and gave her a new focus for her future—to become a professional coach for others.

Moving into several new roles was exciting, and the opportunity to use her new coaching skills was becoming more real every day as she closed out the final days in the public school setting. During Rosemary's final year, she enrolled in coach-skill training and gradually began her work as a new coach. She was called on to help a friend who was faced with downsizing a business during some rough economic times. Downsizing the business was necessary to survive, but this business owner had to lay off an employee who was highly valued and appreciated.

Rosemary, now the coach, used her many new coaching skills to encourage her friend to think in alternative ways during this business transition and to develop a plan not only to create the meeting to announce the layoff but also to plan a severance package for her employee.

Taking time to think through these rough transitions made even the inevitable become more palatable. Allowing planning time and decision-making enabled her friend to make wiser decisions as an employer, and she became very creative with the severance plan. You see, the severance plan not only contained a monetary sum, but it also offered the employee several hours of coaching to ease the employee's job transition. These hours were spent dealing with the loss of a job, preparing for the next position, and even the preparation of a resume. The employer really showed caring and concern for a valued employee through this extension of a severance package and investment in the former employee.

*(Continued)*

(Continued)

Not only did Rosemary make smooth transitions with the help of coaching, but two more people directly benefited through this gift we call coaching conversations. Slowing down to think deeper always allows us to consider our ways and helps create a more purposeful next step in decision-making. Rosemary, who once invested in the growth and development of many teachers in her district, had now expanded her life skills to include coaching, and she was helping friends adjust to life's transitional moments as well as her own.

## Coaching Insights

Individual coaching helped Rosemary discover new possibilities for work after her retirement as an educator. As Rosemary practiced the essential coaching skills of committed listening, paraphrasing, expressing positive intent by asking powerful open-ended questions, and reflective feedback, she not only strengthened her own coach-leader skills, but she also helped a friend and her friend's employee make successful life transitions, too.

Just as a pebble tossed into a pond causes ripples all the way to the edges of the pond, the use of coach-leader skills may touch others far beyond the immediate impact.

---

### Key Ideas for Navigating Life Transitions

- Use committed listening and silence.
- Pose open-ended questions that generate reflection about possibilities and opportunities that exist when thinking about transitions.
- Presume positive intent that the person thinking about life's transitions has the ability and willingness to develop his or her own solutions and plans.
- Provide support and encouragement for solutions by others through reflective feedback.
- Avoid giving advice to others.

## Your Learning

1. Which parts of these stories resonate with you? Why?

2. What life transitions are you or others close to you grappling with right now?

3. What resources might you call upon as you navigate transitions?

_____

_____

_____

_____

_____

_____

_____

_____

_____

_____

_____

_____

_____

_____

_____

_____

_____

# Taking Up the Challenge

### *How Ready Are You to Become a Coach-Leader?*

> *While no conversation is guaranteed to change the trajectory of a career, a relationship, or a life—any single conversation can.*
>
> —Susan Scott, *Fierce Conversations*

Our purpose in writing *Opening the Door to Coaching Conversations* was to demonstrate how leaders resolve common work-related challenges using coaching conversations. Each of the stories' "star" leaders approached his or her issue with a "coaching mindset." Our colleague, Edna Harris, explains that mindset is our attitude, our beliefs, and our way of approaching life. Harris says that with a coaching mindset, leaders believe that people have noble purpose and intent—that they want to be responsible, dependable, and competent. Coach-leaders believe the best in people until they demonstrate otherwise. This creates an environment of trust in which the coach-leader can hold up high expectations as the structure or boundaries within the system.

Coach-leaders address other people as if they have experience, knowledge, and skills to make needed changes. Coach-leaders often set the framework for change by holding up clear standards, criteria, or expectations. Then they negotiate with the staff about how to get the job done in specific situations. They focus on listening intently to understand the perceptions and thinking of others. They also provide resources and multiple options for the ideas that emerge.

Coach-leaders believe in the ability of others to grow and excel. Another colleague, Karen Anderson, wisely observes that by offering full presence, deep listening, and authentic responses, coach-leaders build the efficacy and confidence of others.

Coach-leaders want to be perceived by others as *partners* in change—not experts with all the answers. For this reason, they recognize that advice is toxic. It denigrates a person's intelligence and poisons self-esteem. Instead, coach-leaders ask powerful, open-ended questions that push thinking forward and expose options for consideration.

By operating in this way, coach-leaders draw out the best in people while building high trust and rapport with staff. They know they can always become more forceful and directive if they need to be. But if they start working with people as the *expert problem-solver* and the *answer person,* it is much harder to move into a collaborative and coach-like mode.

> With a coaching mindset, leaders create an environment of trust.

With a coaching mindset, leaders create an environment of trust. Within that environment, they practice four essential communication skills: committed listening, paraphrasing, positive intent, and reflective feedback.

We hope you have seen that committed listening is a powerful tool used by all the leaders in our stories. By listening deeply, without thinking about responses or solutions, the leaders began to clearly understand the points of view, aspirations, and dreams of others. Then they used that information to build rapport, trust, and reflective thinking.

Although in the stories you could not hear the specific paraphrasing language used by the coach-leaders, know that *statements*, not questions, can be very powerful in moving the thinking of others. Statements using the speaker's own language ("You said . . .") or statements that categorize or label something the speaker said ("So you are seeing these things as *barriers* . . .") can be very powerful in moving the thinking of the other person forward. Paraphrasing shows that you are listening and trying to understand.

In each of the stories, the positive intent of the coach-leader is very obvious. When the coach-leader is most successful, he or she assumes that other people are good thinkers and solution seekers, and others have the ability to resolve issues on their own. By working together, they can find even better solutions more quickly.

It is positive intent that helps create the trust environment. It is positive intent that communicates confidence in the skills of the other person. It is positive intent that holds the responsibility for the solution in the lap of the person who owns the problem. The coach-leader helps the person with the issue *think about* how best to resolve it. But the responsibility for action stays with the person who has the issue.

The fourth essential coaching skill, reflective feedback, was demonstrated when coach-leaders in the stories asked those powerful questions. Often the questions were very simple, but they had a powerful effect on the thinking of the other person. They were open-ended, assumed positive intent, and led to action on the part of the thinker.

Many times the questions asked the thinker to compare one situation in which there had been a positive result to the current situation. Statements that lifted up the thinker's strengths often preceded the question—"You were very collaborative with the staff when you had them resolve that staffing issue. How might you use collaboration in this situation?" This helps the thinker view the issue from a specific lens coming from his or her strengths. It helps the thinker consider adapting a prior success to find a current solution.

A simple question can lead to a powerful insight. Asking, "What do you want?" or "What will that look like?" are examples of this. Any question that helps the thinker consider an issue from a new or different vantage point is a good question. It helps the thinker clarify the issues and opens new options for consideration. We know from David Rock's (2006) research that once the thinker has burst with an *aha*, it is time to push for action. The very point of having coaching conversations is to commit to action that leads to the desired results.

We hope these stories have inspired you to practice coach-leadership. By being a leader with a coaching mindset who uses the essential tools of coaching conversations, you can effectively resolve almost any challenge that arises in your school.

# Appendix: Powerful Questions

## *Open-Ended Questions Showing Positive Intent*

### PLANNING A CHANGE

- ☐ What do you want?
- ☐ What does it look like? Sound like?
- ☐ What opportunities does this situation present for you?
- ☐ What are your plans?
- ☐ With whom is it important to share your ideas?
- ☐ What are the anticipated results of . . . ?
- ☐ What is the purpose of . . . ?
- ☐ What are the next steps to continue implementation?

### EXPLORATION OF IDEAS

- ☐ How is this different from . . . ?
- ☐ How will you know if . . . makes a difference?
- ☐ What criteria will you use to judge success?

☐ How do you show support for . . . ?

☐ How will you know students are improving?

☐ How will you get parents involved?

☐ How do you know students understand the expected outcome(s)?

☐ What strengths do you see in . . . ?

☐ What would a trusted friend tell you?

☐ How do you teach that concept and what will students be doing?

☐ What solution do you see as best for students?

☐ I wonder what would happen if . . . ?

☐ What strategies are you considering?

☐ How will you prioritize the work in a proactive way?

☐ What are the actions you directly control upon which you could focus your energy?

☐ Why had one group done this . . . and another group had not?

☐ What alternatives could you use with these children?

☐ How will you know students have mastered a concept?

## DEBRIEFING A SITUATION

☐ How are you doing as a team?

☐ What helped you be successful?

☐ How will you continue to improve?

☐ What do you want in place for next year?

☐ What will you do differently as a result of your insight?

☐ What are ways you could use those skills and apply them to a new situation?

❑ What are changes you have been thinking about that you want to make?

❑ When you reflect on . . . , what are the key elements?

❑ What made the situation successful or not?

❑ If you had been a participant in that situation, what would you have liked the leader to do?

# References

Blanchard, K., Oncken Jr., W., & Burrows, H. (1989). *The one minute manager meets the monkey*. New York: Quill/William Morrow.

Block, P. (2009). *Community: The structure of belonging*. San Francisco: Berrett-Koehler.

Bryk, A. & Schneider, B. (2002). *Trust in schools: A core resource for improvement*. New York: Russell Sage Foundation Pub.

Cheliotes, L. & Reilly, M. (2010). *Coaching conversations: Transforming your school one conversation at a time*. Thousand Oaks, CA: Corwin.

Coaching For Results Global (2011). *Coaching strategies for powerful leading*. Hoyt, KS: Coaching For Results, Inc.

Covey, S. (1990). *The 7 habits of highly effective people*. New York: Fireside.

Dyer, K. & Carothers, J. (2000). *The intuitive principal*. Thousand Oaks, CA: Corwin.

Guskey, T. (2000). *Evaluation of staff development*, Thousand Oaks, CA: Corwin.

Hargreaves, A. & Shirley, D. (2009). *The fourth way*. Thousand Oaks, CA: Corwin.

Heath, C. & Heath, D. (2008). *Made to stick*. New York: Random House.

Kee, K., Anderson, K., Dearing, V., Harris, E., & Shuster, F. (2010). *Results coaching: The new essential for school leaders*. Thousand Oaks, CA: Corwin.

Kouzes, J. & Posner, B. (2002). *The leadership challenge* (3rd ed.). San Francisco: Jossey-Bass.

Lencioni, P. (2002). *The five dysfunctions of a team: A leadership fable*. San Francisco: Jossey-Bass.

Lencioni, P. (2005). Overcoming the five dysfunctions of a team: A field guide for leaders, managers, and facilitators. San Francisco: Jossey-Bass.

Maxwell, J. (2002). *The 17 essential qualities of a team player*. Nashville, TN: Thomas Nelson, Inc.

Orem, S., Binkert, J., & Clancy, A. (2007). *Appreciative coaching.* San Francisco: Jossey-Bass.

Perkins, D. (2003). *King Arthur's roundtable: How collaborative conversations create smart organizations.* Hoboken, NJ: John Wiley and Sons.

Pink, D. (2009). *Drive: The surprising truth about what motivates us.* New York: Penguin Group.

Ramsey, R., (1999). *Lead, follow, or get out of the way.* Thousand Oaks, CA: Corwin.

Rock, D, (2006). *Quiet leadership.* New York: HarperCollins.

Scott, S. (2004). *Fierce conversations.* New York: Berkley Books.

Senge, P., Cambron-McCabe, N., Lucas, T., Smith, B., Dutton, J., & Kleiner, A. (2000). *Schools that learn.* New York: Currency.

Williams, D., & Richardson, E. (2010). *The elementary principal's personal coach.* Thousand Oaks, CA: Corwin.

Zerfoss, D. (2011). *Stress is a choice.* Naperville, IL: Simple Truths.

Ziglar, Z. (2008). *Inspiration 365 days a year.* Naperville, IL: Simple Truths.

# Index

**CORWIN**
A SAGE Company

The Corwin logo—a raven striding across an open book—represents the union of courage and learning. Corwin is committed to improving education for all learners by publishing books and other professional development resources for those serving the field of PreK–12 education. By providing practical, hands-on materials, Corwin continues to carry out the promise of its motto: **"Helping Educators Do Their Work Better."**